Heidi Boyd

Exploring Resin Jewelry

SIMPLE TECHNIQUES FOR 25 PROJECTS

NORTH LIGHT BOOKS
Cincinnati, Ohio

www.CreateMixedMedia.com

CONTENTS

INTRODUCTION

Resin is that irresistible drop of clear plastic that beautifully magnifies a tiny treasure or image. You've seen it in hundreds of commercially made jewelry pieces or in stunning one-of-a-kind creations featured on Etsy, in craft shows, or in galleries.

Very simply, resin is a polymer plastic that requires the precise mixing of a two-part formula. It is poured into a bezel or mold and will cure to a clear hard plastic within twenty-four hours. A highly versatile medium, it lends itself to being layered, drilled, tinted or embedded with objects.

Before embarking on this book I had only dabbled with resin. Like many crafters, I craved the results of crystal-clear resin, but I was turned off by the smell and caustic toxicity of the medium. After immersing myself in the subject, reading and experimenting, I quickly discovered that new compounds and products have resolved the negative associations. Some of the new formulations have virtually no smell, mix easily, and are not harmful to your skin.

My goal in writing this book is to make resin approachable and easy for any beginner. Before you try making your first piece, take some time to read through the resin materials and techniques section. I'll walk you through how to prepare your project and work surface, and how to mix the featured varieties of resin. Armed with basic resin knowledge, you'll be amazed at how easy it is to pour sets of bezels, eliminate pesky air bubbles, embed treasures, and showcase your favorite imagery. I've also included basic jewelry-making techniques so that you can immediately transform your newly made resin creations into wearable pendants, charms and earrings.

When designing projects for this book, my goal was to showcase a diverse array of accessories and materials to motivate beginners and to give experienced resin artists new inspiration. Relishing the element of surprise, I embedded everything from circuitry, candy, postage stamps, shells and butterfly wings to cut-up credit cards in the liquid resin. I also tinted the resin with both transparent and opaque dyes to completely change its appearance. In a few projects we'll try Lisa Pavelka's no-mix resin, which cures when exposed to UV light, and Sherri Haab's unique two-part KlayResin, which quickly cures after mixing.

My hope is that this book will set you on a new course of creativity and that you'll come back to it again and again for inspiration. The best part of resin jewelry making is that after you make one of these beauties, you'll be able to share the joy and gift them to special friends or proudly wear them yourself.

RESIN MATERIALS AND TECHNIQUES

Take a moment to read over these techniques. These vital steps will guide you through safely pouring, finishing, and fixing problems with a resin creation, and reveal all the tricks and tips that I've discovered by trial and error. The individual project instructions will refer you back to these details. Take advantage of my experience and benefit from my mistakes.

SELECTING AND PREPARING ITEMS TO EMBED IN RESIN

paper

Photos and designs printed on paper are the most popular items to be trapped in resin. Resin is readily absorbed into paper and will darken it and give it a transparent look (much like if you spilled water on it). So, unless you are seeking a transparent appearance for your design (such as in *Resin Paper Earrings* on page 69), you'll need to protect your image with brush-on sealer or clear packing tape. Here's how:

Protecting with sealer. Working over wax paper, apply three coats of an acrylic découpage medium, such as Mod Podge (PLAID), to both sides (and the edges) of your cut paper. Let each layer dry before applying the next one. Make sure the piece fully dries overnight before placing it in the resin. If you're placing the paper in a bezel, use Mod Podge as glue to set it in the bezel, and then spread another coat over the top and sides to further secure it in place.

Protecting with packing tape. It's so quick and easy to simply trap the cut paper between two layers of clear packing tape. Use a bone folder or burnishing stick to tightly seal the tape layers over and around the image. Using scissors, trim away excess tape from the edges of the image. Be careful not to cut too close and make a hole in the sealed tape. If you're concerned that resin may seep in, apply a thin bead of craft glue along the cut tape edge.

In one project (Butterfly Beauty Pendant, page 111), I had trouble spray-coating butterfly wings with acrylic. The force of the spray made them fly across the room. I had more success using Mod Podge to attach the small wing pieces directly onto paper to seal them.

If you're printing an image from your computer, let the printed ink dry completely (overnight) before sealing it. I ruined some beautiful images by prematurely brushing sealer onto the photo paper. The red ink in particular smeared and tinted the image.

found objects

Almost anything that is small enough to place in your bezel or mold can be trapped in resin. Nonporous items such as small metal charms, watch parts, plastic toys, shells, game pieces, sequins, beads and buttons are all acceptable inclusions. As long as they're clean and completely dry, they're ready to use. To prevent air bubbles from forming, brush each item with a coat of resin just before submerging it into the mold or bezel.

natural items (and candy)

Any item that may contain residual moisture—like dried flowers, bugs, butterfly wings, wood, leaves or candy pieces—may need a protective coat of acrylic spray to prevent moisture or color from leeching out into the resin. As an extra preventative, you can place natural items in silica gel to help draw out any moisture before sealing them in acrylic.

fabric

You may have success placing fabric and fibers directly into resin. With the *Keep-the-Piece Fabric Pendant* (page 107), I was concerned that the vibrant colors in the unwashed cotton might leech out, so I sealed the back and front of the fabric piece with layers of Mod Podge découpage medium. This gave it sturdiness and made the piece easier to handle, coat with resin, and place into the mold.

SELECTING AND PREPARING YOUR MOLDS

Purchase molds intended for resin. They're available at craft stores and through online suppliers, in assorted shapes and sizes (they even come in variety trays). You can also use food-safe silicone molds; the ice cube variety are perfectly sized for jewelry making. Be sure that you dedicate your mold for resin and do not cook food in it before or after using it for resin.

It's also surprisingly easy to make your own mold with Castin' Craft EasyMold Silicone Putty (see *Cute as a Button Earrings* on page 93 and *Hootenanny Bracelet* on page 98).

The first step in preparing a mold for pouring is to make sure it's dust free. Spray with Mold Release (Castin' Craft) and carefully follow the package instructions to ensure it's completely dry before mixing your resin. An intricate mold may require a second coat of spray.

PREPARING YOUR BEZELS

Bezels are usually made of metal and are shaped like tiny pans with raised sides and a hanging loop. They're ideal for resin because the sides of the bezel trap liquid resin. They come in a variety of shapes and sizes. Pricing depends on the precious metal content and weight. Look for specialty ring and earring bezels.

Once you've properly anchored an image in your bezel (see *Protecting with sealer*, page 6), push the back of the ring down into a block of floral foam so that it supports the bezel and holds it level. If you're using a pendant bezel, check if the hanging loop dips below the bezel pan. If it does, let the loop hang over the edge of the block so that the bezel portion is level.

If you're concerned about protecting the finish of your metal bezel, wrap the edge in clear adhesive tape.

PREPARING YOUR WORKSPACE

Mixing resin reminds me of cooking—you need to assemble all the necessary ingredients before you start. It's critical to read the recipe and carefully follow the instructions. With a little practice, it's as easy as pie!

ventilation

Good ventilation is a necessity for resin. Even if you can't smell the fumes, you're mixing chemicals together and there will be off-gassing. Working outside is great, a ventilated studio ideal; in a traditional home, be sure to open your windows and turn on a fan. In the cool climate of Maine where I live, it's easier to meet ventilation and temperature requirements in the summer and early autumn.

room temperature

Resin needs adequate warmth to properly cure. Seventy degrees appears to be the magic number with most formulas. The warmer the temperature, the faster the resin will cure. Excess heat or overwarming the formulas before or after mixing may limit your window for embedding objects or removing bubbles. Check the resin package instructions for proper storage; unused formulas should not be left out in the cold.

work area

Most resin packaging recommends that you mix resin away from where you prepare foods. They want to ensure that you won't contaminate your food preparation areas with toxic resin. Cured resin is almost impossible to remove from your counters or sink. Taking their precautions to heart, I still chose to work in my kitchen. It has great ventilation, good lighting, electrical outlets for the heat gun, a timer, and a sink for hot water baths when needed. I laid down wooden boards over my countertops and covered them with sheets of wax paper. I set up a curing space in an adjacent room with desk lamps for additional heat, and dust covers so that the poured resin could cure undisturbed.

time-sensitivity

Once you begin mixing resin, the clock starts ticking. You have approximately a 10-to-20-minute window to pour the liquid resin into molds or bezels and embed your inclusions. Try to minimize any distractions. Choose a time when children and spouses or roommates are out, and turn off your phone. Make sure you've prepared your work area by ventilating the room, adjusting the heat, setting out your molds (or bezels), and assembling all the necessary supplies (see *Basic mixing and pouring materials*, next page). You don't want to be hunting down stirring sticks while your unmixed resin is hardening. Be sure to arrange all of your equipment within easy reach on your wax-papered work surface.

basic mixing and pouring materials

Once a tool has been dipped in resin, it's ruined. For that reason use inexpensive, disposable items to mix and pour resin. Don't sacrifice your favorite tweezers or paintbrushes. Traditional solvents won't affect cured resin. Some resin suppliers such as Little Windows sell nifty little plastic stirrers, and ICE resin has great disposable bottles with squeeze tops for dripping liquid resin into molds. Avoid using paper products or wax paper cups, which will disintegrate. Be sure to arrange all of your equipment within easy reach on your wax-papered work surface, including the following items.

Timer. It's vital to have a clock or timer close at hand, as most resin formulas call for two separate timed stirring sessions.

Natural wood craft sticks for mixing the two-part resin formulas together.

Natural wood toothpicks for positioning items, dripping resin into small spaces and popping bubbles.

Calibrated disposable measuring cups, like the ones sold with cough syrup; 1- to 12-ounce cups are sold with resin supplies.

Inexpensive paintbrushes like those in kids' painting kits. They're sold in economy-sized bags in craft stores. Use them for coating inclusions, and for top finish coats.

Baby wipes are fabulous for cleaning the edges of bezels or wiping up spills. They immediately cut the oil and wipe away stickiness. Don't substitute paper towels that will just stick to the mess.

Nitrile disposable gloves are vital if you're using Castin' Craft resin and dyes.

Safety glasses. Trust me, you don't want liquid resin splashing into your eyes.

A low-temperature heat gun instantly removes air bubbles from curing resin (blowing through a straw is a low-tech substitute, but not as effective).

Straight pins for small positioning adjustments or bubble popping.

Bent tweezers, for placing items into resin. Try to avoid getting resin on the tips; use baby wipes to quickly wipe any off. If allowed to cure, your calipers won't open, rendering them useless.

additional tools & supplies needed for projects

Sharp craft scissors, scalloped decorative scissors, craft knife, razor blade

Circle cutters (sizes vary)

Bone folder (or paintbrush handle)

Computer and printer with glossy photo paper

Clear packing tape, double-sided tape, metal adhesive tape

Clear transparency or shrink plastic sheet

Polymer clay (white, shimmery white)

Acrylic paint (silver metallic)

Copper pipe

Pipe cutter

Drill with ⅛" (3mm) and ¹⁄₁₆" (2mm) bits

Craft oven (or toaster oven used only for baking polymer clay), baking tile

Pasta machine

Rubber mallet

PROPER MEASURING AND MIXING TECHNIQUES

Prepare your space and assemble all the materials you'll need before mixing your resin. Be sure to read through each resin's package instructions before you begin, as manufacturers include important information pertinent to their product.

Be sure to set your timer anytime you must stir or let the resin sit for a certain period of time, and stick strictly to the amounts of time given.

castin' craft resin

Sold as EasyCast Clear Casting Epoxy, this product has been on the craft market for a long time, is competitively priced, and is widely available. I like to use it for projects that require a large amount of resin. It's vital to pull on your gloves and keep them on the entire time you work with Castin' Craft resin. **Direct contact with your skin is harmful.** Make sure the room is well-ventilated, and wear a respirator mask if possible.

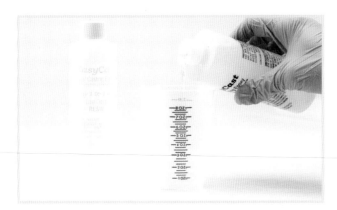

1 Pour the formula from bottle A into a calibrated cup and then add an equal amount from bottle B.

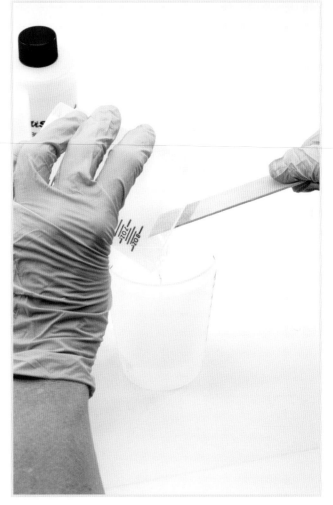

2 Use a craft stick to stir the two parts together for exactly 2 minutes. Be sure to agitate the entire solution, scraping the bottom and sides of the cup. Use a consistent motion to blend the two parts, but avoid whipping them into a frenzy of bubbles.

3 Pour the blended solution into a new cup and switch to a new stick. Stir the mixture for another full minute. Then allow the solution to sit for a minute so the majority of the bubbles dissipate.

ice resin

Susan Lenart Kazmer developed ICE resin to use in her stunning mixed-media jewelry creations. The resulting product is so successful and easy to use that it's become incredibly popular with both artists and crafters. It's available in small 1-ounce double-plunger form, ideal for pouring a set of bezels, or in larger bottles. It has virtually no smell, and direct contact should not harm your skin. It will leave a sticky residue that can be removed with baby wipes. Pumice hand cleaners sold at automotive stores are great for removing the stickiness from under your nails.

1 Prewarm the containers in a warm water bath (float in the kitchen sink). This step will help prevent air bubbles from forming later. Be careful not to overwarm the bottles, which will cause the resin to cure quickly and shorten your working time.

2 Pour equal parts of the two-part formula into a calibrated cup. Pour part A first.

3 Then pour part B into the cup.

4 Use a craft stick to stir the solution for 2 minutes. You'll see the two parts swirling together; once properly blended, you won't be able to discern any striations. Let the mixture sit for 5 minutes to allow any bubbles to dissipate.

little windows resin

Fran Valera first developed her crystal-clear Little Windows resin to showcase photographs in jewelry. Her proprietary resin is very stable, cures at a consistent internal temperature, forms almost no bubbles in mixing, has virtually no odor, and will not irritate your skin (remove stickiness with baby wipes). Because of all these factors, it is also gaining popularity with mixed-media artists and crafters. I chose to use it for almost all the image and photography projects in this book.

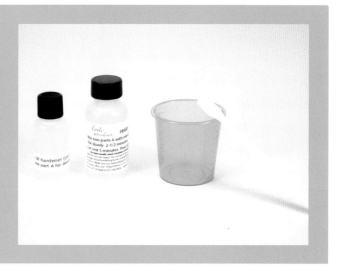

1 Little Windows requires a 2-to-1 ratio (A:B). Pour part A first. (It's helpful to premark your pouring amount on the cup.)

2 Add part B, up to the second line you've premarked.

3 Stir the solution for 2½ minutes, scraping the sides and bottom to mix thoroughly. Try not to create any bubbles while stirring. Let it sit for 5 minutes before pouring.

ADDING COLOR TO RESIN

Coloring resin immediately changes its appearance from crystal clear into a solid-colored creation. There are degrees to coloring. Start with a simple project that has floating specks of color. Next, try adding small amounts of transparent or opaque colorants to another batch of resin (see *Faux Sea Glass Pendant* on page 89). Finally, test the possibilities by making a project that swirls two colors together or layers a new color over a cured color (see *Butterfly Beauty Pendant* on page 111).

The key to successfully tinting resin is to avoid altering the formula with moisture—which means adding dry colorants, oil paints or specially formulated dyes into liquid resin, or coloring cured resin with alcohol inks.

Colored resin does not change its appearance when it cures, so start light and slowly add color, and stop when you're happy with the hue.

dry colorants

Powdered spices can be added to liquid resin to give it a natural speckled coloring.

Grated chalk pastel dust will provide a vibrant, cloudy appearance.

Pearl Ex powdered pigments have the most dramatic effect. Just a small pinch will transform the resin into a glittery colored cloud.

wet colorants

Oil paints. The smallest squeeze of oil paint will color a great deal of liquid resin. Make sure you take the time to completely integrate it into the resin. To make any oil color opaque, add a small touch of white paint.

Pigments and dyes. Castin' Craft has a full line of liquid colors that readily mix into resin. Much like food coloring, a single drop or two goes a long way. Castin' Craft dyes are divided into two varieties: opaque pigments and transparent dyes.

Alcohol inks. Sold with rubber stamping products, alcohol inks can be directly applied to cured resin. Wipe away the excess and reapply until you're pleased with the results.

StazOn permanent stamp pad. Rubber stamping permanent ink directly onto cured resin is another way to add color.

POURING

If you're using small, calibrated mixing cups, it should be fairly easy to pour the solution directly from the cup into a mold or bezel. If you need to fill a small space, you can drip the resin from the end of a craft stick or toothpick, or transfer the resin to a disposable squeeze bottle.

The key to successful pouring is not to overfill. Let the liquid resin settle into the mold or bezel. You can tilt the piece from side to side to force the resin around inclusions. You can also use the tip of a toothpick to coax the resin into position. Once the resin has leveled, add a drop or two more if necessary to bring the resin right up to the lip of the mold or bezel. If any resin drips over the edge of the bezel, use a baby wipe to immediately wipe it away; paper towels will just stick.

Intricate silicone molds, like those used in the *Cute as a Button Earrings* (page 93) and *Hootenanny Bracelet* (page 98) projects, require an extra step. You need to use a paintbrush to force the resin into the tiny nooks and crevices of the mold. Otherwise, trapped air bubbles will create holes in your creation.

DOMING

A dome is that beautiful rounded resin top and is often the result of multiple pours (with twenty-four hours of drying time in between). Once in a while you'll get lucky and the resin will dome in a single pour without dripping over the sides of the bezel. This miracle happened for me when I worked on the *Short Circuit Pendant* (page 29) and the *Cheeky Double-Sided Earrings* (page 65). Other pieces like the *Timeless Steampunk Pendant* (page 57) and the *Bubble Rings* (page 36) took several pourings to achieve a luscious dome.

BUBBLE CONTROL

The first step in bubble control is to carefully follow the resin product's mixing instructions and have the formula at the proper temperature. Letting the mixed solution rest for several minutes will allow some bubbles to dissipate before you pour the resin. The following strategies will help you remove bubbles from poured resin.

Once the surface of the resin has hardened, you've missed the opportunity to remove bubbles. Be sure to keep an eye on your poured pieces as they begin to set up.

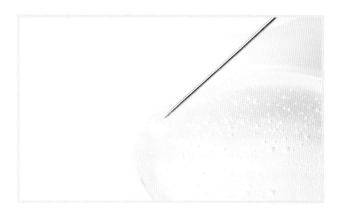

Popping with a straight pin will quickly eliminate a bubble, but agitating the surface of the resin can also create more bubbles. Keep an eye on the piece to make sure other bubbles don't form.

Exhaling through a straw may assist in popping a bubble or two. The directed combination of warmth and carbon does the trick. Just don't inhale!

Placing a desk lamp over curing resin will help disperse bubbles. The lamp provides direct warmth that draws bubbles to the surface.

A low-temperature heat gun (not to be confused with an embossing heat gun) is well worth the small investment for resin work. It has a slow-speed fan that skims the surface of the resin and immediately pops every bubble—even the pesky, tiny hard-to-see ones. While making the jewelry in this book, I skimmed each piece to ensure it was bubble free.

DRYING/CURING

Make sure you cure your poured resin on a level surface. I once placed a freshly filled mold tray on top of a stack of books, out of reach of kids and pets, without realizing that the tray wasn't level. The resin cured slanted, thin on one side and deep on the other.

In colder climates, simply placing desk lamps over curing resin helps keep the resin at an ideal warm temperature.

Dust is all around us, and uncured resin does a wonderful job of catching those particles and encasing them. Simply placing an inverted plastic storage container over your work will prevent this attraction. (Be sure to rest the base of the tub on blocks/books so that air can still flow around the pieces.) This is especially important if you're working outdoors, to protect your pieces from pollen dust and windblown plant and tree debris.

UNMOLDING

The trick to successful unmolding is to make sure the resin is fully cured and the mold was properly prepared with mold release spray. If a piece refuses to pop out of its mold, stick the whole thing in the freezer for a few minutes; that should pop it right out. Don't attempt to pick up the piece with sharp tools; instead, exert pressure from the underside of the flexible mold.

SANDING

Often resin work doesn't require any sanding, but in some projects, like the *Credit on Ice Bangles* (page 76) and the *Faux Sea Glass Pendant* (page 89), require a great deal of sanding.

The first step is to cut away any of the overpour of the unmolded piece with sharp craft scissors. Then you can begin sanding.

Emery boards are ideal for small sanding jobs; their shape allows them to fit into openings, and their rigidity helps quickly smooth rough edges. For more elaborate sanding, purchase an assortment of wet/dry sandpapers meant for automotive plastic. Begin with coarse 300-grit, work your way up to 400-grit, and then use fine 600-grit for final polishing. To prevent harmful resin dust from being inhaled or ingested, wear a mask if you dry-sand the piece. Sanding your piece while it's underwater will keep airborne resin dust at a minimum. I found it helpful to tear off small sections of sandpaper and label the grit number on the back.

FINISHING POURED BEZEL PIECES

Sometimes cured drips will require painstaking sanding and cleaning up, which may damage the finish of your bezel. Other times the overspill will easily peel right off of the bezel. The trick is cleaning the piece when it's freshly cured (don't rush it; make sure it's fully hardened). The longer it sits, the more stubborn the adhesion to the metal.

I ruined the finish on a ring (shown on this page) by leaving it too long in floral foam. When I finally pulled it out of the foam, I couldn't pull off the overspill and ended up having to sand off the hardened resin, damaging the ring's finish.

Even when you follow all the steps and do everything right, you might find something went wrong and there's a bubble in the middle of your once-perfect creation. Have no fear—it can be fixed! Be sure the resin is completely cured before you sand away the offending bubble. A Dremel rotary tool with a sanding attachment is very adept at this procedure. Wash and dry the piece before repouring a new resin top. You'll be amazed at how you won't be able to see the connection between the new and old pourings.

tip

DRILLING CURED PIECES

The small size and adjustable speed of the Dremel rotary tool makes it easy to handle. Arm yourself with ⅛" (3mm) and ¹⁄₁₆" (2mm) drill bits to make stringing holes in your resin pieces. Like sanding, drilling resin generates harmful resin dust, so be sure to wear a respiratory mask and protective eyewear. Working over a small piece of scrap wood, drill a hole straight through your cured piece. If you're not comfortable holding the piece with your fingertips, you can anchor it in a vice.

When drilling through a clear resin piece, the drilled interior portion will become opaque with the abrasion. Follow the steps for topcoating (below) to coat the inside of the hole with a fine coat of resin; this will restore the drilled hole to its original crystal-clear appearance.

FINISHING TECHNIQUES

Post-sanding/drilling resin topcoat. After sanding your resin piece with fine (600-grit) sandpaper, wash away loose dust and let the piece dry. Then stick the base to a piece of clear packing tape, rubbing it firmly onto the base and up against the bottom edge. The tape will anchor the cured resin while you brush on a thin topcoat of liquid resin (it will also stop any drips from sliding under the piece). Mix a small amount of resin and use a disposable paintbrush to apply a thin coat over the top of your piece. Let the piece fully cure before removing the tape.

Zap-A-Gap glue came with my designer kit from Little Windows. It's a superglue formula that instantly bonds resin pieces to metal, or resin to itself. It comes with an interchangeable tiny tip that is great for getting into tight areas. In a pinch, it will fix or seal a hole in your resin piece. Watch your fingertips, though; this adhesive bonds so quickly that if you're not careful, it'll bond your fingertips to your jewelry!

Crystal Clear Carnauba wax, sold in the automotive section for polishing plastic interior car parts, is often suggested for polishing sanded resin pieces. I can see the appeal—it's a quick solution: just squeeze a drop onto a rag and rub it over the piece. Use a clean cloth to rub away the wax and shine. The drawback is that it doesn't replace the original clarity—it leaves the resin with a slightly dull or cloudy finish.

tip

If you need to make a hole through a slim piece of resin, Little Windows sells a tiny handheld tool that you rotate in the palm of your hand.

Remember, you can always sand it and fix it! "Craft-astrophes" happen all the time. Fortunately, resin is surprisingly fixable. If something falls over, dries unevenly, or develops unsightly bumps, let the resin cure and then follow the steps presented previously to sand away the problem and repour a shiny new coat over the top.

JEWELRY-MAKING TECHNIQUES

Jewelry making looks complicated to those who haven't tried it, but it's not. You'll be amazed at how simple these basic techniques are, and how quick and satisfying it is to transform your cured resin pieces into jewelry. Even if you're an experienced jewelry maker, you may not have tied cording into an overhand knot, or used foldover crimps to finish suede lace ends—skills that are useful for making your own jewelry cords to wear your resin pendants. These techniques and a few other basics are presented here, and additional ones will be introduced as you work your way through the book.

jewelry-making tools & supplies needed for projects

Pliers: needle-nose, chain-nose, round-nose, bent-nose, crimping

Flush cutters

Bent tweezers

Ring mandrel (or dowel rod)

Jeweler's hammer

Metal bench block

Jewelry glue

Types and sizes are specified in each project when these items are used:

Jewelry hooks, bails

Jump rings, split rings, figure-eight rings

Beads, rhinestones, buttons, charms, findings

Crimps, fold-over crimps, crimp beads

Head pins, eye pins

Earwires

Leather cording, velour cording

Jewelry chains and wire

Stringing wire and rubber tubing

Ribbon

Lobster and spring clasps

Bracelet blanks

CRIMPING A STRINGING WIRE

This basic stringing technique should be the first technique that you learn. Crimping takes the place of knotting; crimps are regularly attached to the end of a beaded strand. A crimp bead is essentially a small wire tube strung onto a cabled stringing wire. When you squeeze the crimp with crimping pliers or chain-nose pliers, it traps the stringing wire in place.

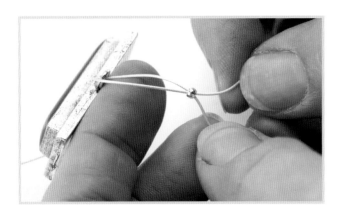

1 String a crimp bead onto a stringing wire. Pass the stringing wire through the hanging loop on the bezel. String the stringing wire back through the crimp bead.

2 Pull through any slack stringing wire and push the bead down flush against the hanging loop or clasp. Use crimping pliers to squeeze the crimp flat. Trim away the excess wire with flush cutters.

OPENING AND CLOSING A JUMP RING

Jump rings are handy connectors. You can use them to hang a finished resin piece from a cord, or to attach a clasp to the end of a chain.

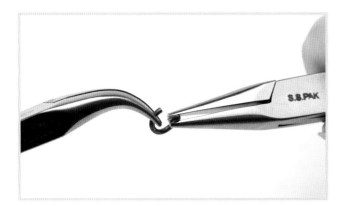

1 Using two pairs of pliers (shown are bent-nose and chain-nose), grab the jump ring on either side of the split. Open the jump ring laterally by exerting pressure in opposite directions, lifting one side of the jump ring up and the other side down. Do not pull the wire ends away from each other, as horizontal action can distort the shape of the jump ring and weaken it.

2 Close the jump ring by using the pliers to return the wire ends to their original position. You can hear or feel a small click when they spring back into position.

MAKING A WRAPPED LOOP AT THE END OF A HEAD PIN

A head pin is a section of straight wire with a small, round head on the end. They're often used for making earrings and beaded dangles.

1 Slide a bead onto a head pin and grab the wire above the bead with round-nose pliers. Bend the wire over the pincer at a 90-degree angle. Create a loop in the wire by wrapping the wire completely around one end of the pincer.

2 Grab the loop with your chain-nose pliers while tightly wrapping the other end of the wire around the base of the loop. Trim away the excess wire with flush cutters.

FOLDING OVER CRIMPS

Fold-over crimps are ideal for finishing the ends of the suede, lace, velour, tubing or ribbon you might use for a necklace or bracelet. The metal ends fold over to trap the fiber ends, and the metal ring allows the finished end to be easily connected to jump rings and clasps.

1 Place the base of the ribbon over the middle of the crimp. Use chain-nose pliers to fold one of the metal tabs over the ribbon end, trapping it against the middle of the crimp.

2 Repeat the process to fold the second metal tab over the first. Use your chain-nose pliers to firmly squeeze the folded crimp, tightening the folds and ensuring that the ribbon won't slip out.

3 Now you can open the ring end of a hook laterally and slip it on the ring end of the crimp to finish the crimped end. Use pliers to return the ring end of the clasp to its original shape.

TYING AN OVERHAND KNOT

Tying an overhand knot is a quick way to form a sturdy loop at the end of your jewelry cord. A lobster clasp or spring clasp can easily hook onto and unhook from the loop. Leather cording is an ideal choice; plastic cording doesn't knot as tightly and tends to loosen.

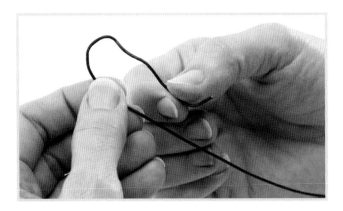

1 Fold over the last couple of inches (several centimeters) of the cording.

2 Holding the top folded loop in one hand and the loose and long cords in the other hand, bring them together to form a circle. Push the loop end up through the middle of the circle.

3 Check the placement and size of the loop before pulling the ends tight. Cut any excess length off the short (loose) end of the cording.

WOODLAND SCRABBLE TILE PENDANTS

These wood pendants are one of the quickest and easiest beginner resin projects. It's easy to see how crafters get hooked on this one and churn out pendant after pendant. There's an endless amount of imagery available online that is sized for Scrabble game tiles. I couldn't resist the simple, vibrant graphic in this woodland sheet from Sparrow Graphics.

1 Print your image sheet off the computer onto glossy photo paper and let the ink dry overnight before applying Mod Podge to prevent the colors from bleeding. Cut out the desired images, trimming away the white background.

materials

ICE resin

Wooden Scrabble tiles (Hasbro)

Tile-sized images (etsy.com/shop/sparrowgraphic)

Glossy photo paper

22" (56cm) 1mm leather cord

Bail, 4mm opening

Lobster clasp

Zip Dry paper glue

Mod Podge découpage medium

Jewelry glue

Small paintbrush

basic resin supplies

Calibrated mixing cups, craft sticks, toothpicks, straight pin, wax paper, lamp for curing

tools

Computer and printer, sharp craft scissors

Finished length:
17½" (44cm) plus ¹³⁄₁₆" (21mm) pendant

2 Use Zip Dry glue to adhere the back of the image to the smooth side of the tile.

tip *Many of the projects in this book require using a strong adhesive such as Zap-A-Gap, but because this one involves affixing paper to wood, Zip Dry paper glue (Beacon Adhesives)—which dries without wrinkling your paper—is the adhesive to use.*

3 Turn each tile over and trim the paper to an exact fit. Clip all 4 corners.

4 Brush 3 coats of Mod Podge over the image and the edges of the paper. Let it dry between coats.

5 Mix the resin (see page 11 for preparation) and arrange the tiles over a sheet of wax paper. Pour a generous amount of resin onto the center of each tile.

6 Use a toothpick to spread the resin to the edges. Apply 1 or 2 more drops of resin to the center to create a dome.

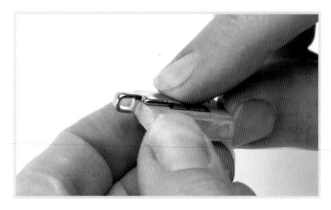

7 After the piece has dried for 24 hours, attach a bail to the back side of the pendant, using jewelry glue.

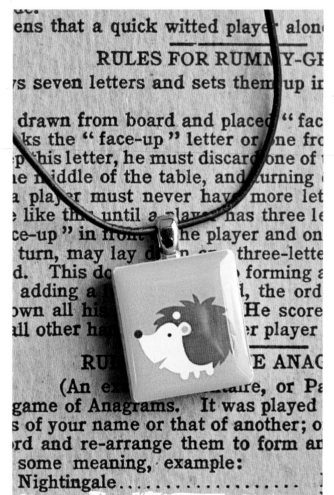

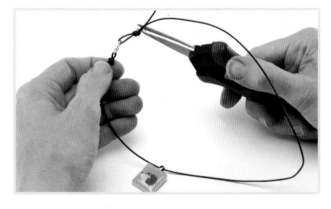

8 String a leather cord through the bail. Tie an overhand knot on each end: one to tie on the lobster clasp, and the other to form a loop for the clasp to grab (see *Tying an overhand knot* on page 21). Trim off the excess cord.

SPOONFUL OF SUGAR CANDY RING

Wearing this playful candy jewelry will surely sweeten your day. It's a calorie-free way to enjoy the vibrant colors of fun-shaped confetti sprinkles. Safely embedded in resin, they'll keep their shape and color and won't melt into frosting.

materials

ICE resin

30mm × 25mm ring bezel (Amate Studios)

Assorted candy sprinkles: Colored and pearl nonpareils, colored sprinkles, flower- and star-shaped confetti

Floral foam block

basic resin supplies

Calibrated mixing cups, craft sticks, toothpicks, straight pin, wax paper, lamp for curing

Finished size:
1 3/16" (30mm) ring face

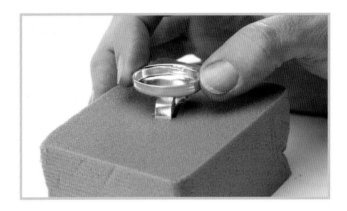

1 Press the ring back into the floral foam so that the bezel is level.

 tip *While it's almost always better to err on the side of being cautious, I found that the candy sprinkles in this project didn't require a protective sealant.*

2 Mix the resin (see page 11 for preparation) and pour a small amount into the bezel.

3 Pour a small amount of the tiny colored nonpareils into the bezel.

4 Tip and rotate the bezel so that the resin coats the bottom.

5 Next, add an assortment of the larger candy balls, confetti and sprinkles. (Avoid brown chocolate sprinkles, which would darken the bright candy color palette.)

6 Drop resin over the arrangement until it is level with the top of the bezel.

7 Use a toothpick to push individual sprinkles into any empty spaces.

8 If any of the candy protrudes past the top of the bezel, push it back into place with the end of the toothpick. As long as the piece isn't too exposed, it will be covered with the next layer of resin. Let the resin fully cure under the lamp for 24 hours.

9 Mix another batch of resin and carefully pour it over the center of the bezel to create a domed top, moving it to the edges with a toothpick.

10 After 24 hours have passed, remove the ring from the foam and clean up the cured resin from under and around the bezel.

POSTS PACK A COLORFUL PUNCH

If large bezel rings aren't your style, try making small post earrings, using just nonpareils or throwing some bigger elements (such as pearls and flower confetti) into the mix.

SHORT CIRCUIT PENDANT

Circuit boards usually hide behind the scenes, busy making the technology in our lives run. My father was a brilliant electrical engineer. I remember checking out his elaborate hand-drawn circuit board images in his study. I say embrace the beauty of technology: cut it out, frame it, and magnify the tiny soldering with resin.

materials

Castin' Craft resin

Old circuit board

37mm × 18mm deep rectangle bezel
(Objects and Elements)

2 10" (25cm) strands of stringing wire

2 7½" (19cm) lengths of rubber tubing (Beadalon)

4 4mm silver beads

4 2mm silver crimps

Opaque colored glass bead, threaded onto an 8mm
jump ring (Industrial Chic by Susan Lenart Kazmer)

Spring clasp

basic resin supplies

Nitrile gloves, calibrated mixing cups, craft sticks,
toothpicks, straight pin, wax paper, lamp for curing

tools

Metal shears (Rings & Things), flush cutters,
crimping pliers

Finished length:
18" (46cm) plus 1⁷⁄₁₆" (37mm) pendant

1 Use the shears to carefully cut a piece of circuit
board to fit inside the bezel (see sidebar).

2 Pour a small amount of resin (see page 10 for
preparation) into the bezel, tipping the bezel to
spread the resin. (Don't skip this part, or air bubbles
may form.) Then coat the circuit board with resin and
place in the bezel. Pour resin over the piece until it
begins to dome. Don't overfill. Let the piece fully cure
under the lamp for 24 hours. *NOTE:* Be sure to wear
your gloves while handling this type of resin.

tip *Use extreme caution when handling
the circuit board, and don't touch any
marked areas that may hold a charge.*

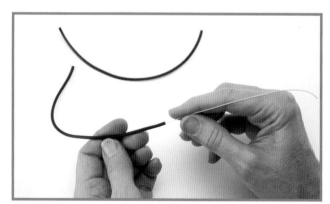

3 Thread each stringing wire through a section of
rubber tubing.

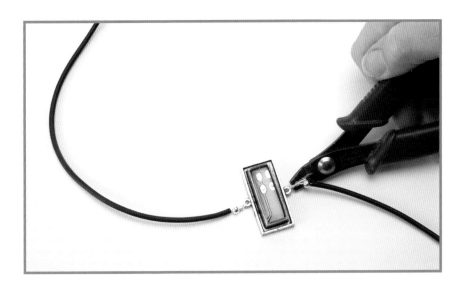

4 String one end of the wire through a silver bead, a crimp, and one of the bezel's hanging loops, then back through the crimp and the bead. Leave enough wire to tuck back into the rubber tubing. Do the same for the other side. Then squeeze the crimp flat on each side of the bezel (see *Crimping a stringing wire* on page 18).

5 String one of the remaining wire ends through another silver bead, a crimp and the metal tab, then back through the crimp and the bead. Squeeze the crimp flat.

6 String the last wire end through a silver bead, a crimp and the jump-ring bead dangle, then back through the crimp and the bead. Squeeze the crimp flat, and add the spring clasp to the jump ring.

FULL CIRCLE

For this design, my husband helped me cut a circular piece of circuit board by using a hole saw attachment on his drill. The Elements bezel brings out the circuitry's round details.

UNCHARTERED BRACELET

I live in Maine, and it's no secret that I love everything about our coastline. The islands are a constant source of fascination, and on marine charts they are perfectly sized to fit into small bezels for a bracelet such as this one. You could easily customize this project to work with vintage or current maps depicting the places you love.

1 Select the section of the map you want to feature in the bezel. If necessary, cut into the map so that the circle cutter can reach the image. Punch out a circle to fit in your bezel (see tip).

2 Coat the front and back of the circle with 3 coats of Mod Podge, drying between coats.

3 Brush Mod Podge inside the bezel, press in the coated paper circle, and seal the top and sides of the circle with a coat of Mod Podge. Let this dry and then recoat.

materials

ICE resin

Marine chart (DeLorme) (could also use atlas pages, vintage or current maps)

22mm circle bezel with loop (Amate Studios)

At least 17" (43cm) of 1mm brown leather cording

Mod Podge découpage medium

Floral foam block

Small paintbrush

basic resin supplies

Calibrated mixing cups, craft sticks, toothpicks, straight pin, wax paper, lamp for curing

tools

13/16" (20mm) circle cutter, sharp craft scissors

Finished size:
14/16" (22mm) bezel; adjustable cord

tip Manufacturers don't always list bezel size, or the interior of the bezel, so fitting a test punch on scrap paper into your bezel is a good idea to make sure you are using the correct-size cutter.

4 Set the bezel on the foam block with its loop hanging off the edge, so the bezel is flat. Then mix the resin (see page 11 for preparation) and pour it into the bezel. Make sure the resin is level with the top of the bezel. Let it cure under the lamp for 24 hours.

5 Apply a second coat of resin to dome the top and let it cure for 24 hours.

tip Use scissors to pull away any floral foam that sticks to the bezel after the resin has dried. Be careful to only grab the cured resin with your scissor tip, to avoid scratching the metal bezel.

6 String the leather cord through the bezel twice, as shown.

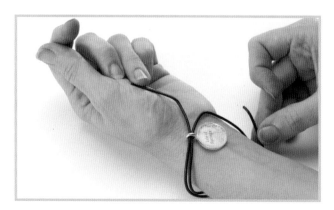

7 Tie one end of the leather cord around the other, and test-fit the bracelet to determine how much length you need for the bracelet to expand over your hand.

8 Trim away the excess cord, and tie the remaining loose end to the cord circle.

LAY ON THE CHARM

If your creation needs a little more sparkle, add a charm that goes with your map. A starfish is ideal for a coastal locale; a cowboy boot or cactus suits a Southwestern spot.

BUBBLE RINGS

These playful rings bring back memories of gumball machine jewelry. Create an eye-catching focal point by layering vintage plastic bead disks over scrapbook paper circles.

1 Use the circle cutter to cut out a focal point from the scrapbook paper for the base of the ring.

materials

Castin' Craft resin

25mm adjustable bezel ring (Amate Studios)

Scrapbook paper, patterned with detailed circle motifs

Vintage plastic flower beads

Mod Podge découpage medium

Zap-A-Gap glue

Floral foam block

Small paintbrush

basic resin supplies

Nitrile gloves, calibrated mixing cups, craft sticks, toothpicks, straight pin, wax paper, lamp for curing

tools

13/16" (20mm) circle cutter

Finished size:
1" (25mm) ring face

2 Coat the front and back of the paper circle with 3 coats of Mod Podge, drying between coats.

3 Brush Mod Podge inside the bezel, and press in the coated paper circle. Seal the top and sides of the circle with a couple of coats of Mod Podge, letting the paper dry between coats.

4 Select and glue plastic beads on top of the center of the paper circle.

5 Press the ring back into the floral foam so that the bezel sits flat and is level. Let the glue used for the plastic beads dry.

6 Mix the resin (see page 10 for preparation) and pour it into the bezel, being careful not to overfill. *NOTE:* Be sure to wear your gloves while handling this type of resin.

7 Cure the ring under the lamp for 24 hours. Then apply another layer of resin to dome the top, and to cover any bead elements that may emerge above the resin surface. Let it cure again for 24 hours.

tip *Miniature plastic toys would make a playful substitute for the beads in this project.*

ONE SHEET, MANY DESIGNS
The single sheet of scrapbook paper I chose offered a great selection of detailed color bursts for coordinating with vintage plastic beads.

JUST MY TYPE BRACELET

This fun bracelet is inspired by the work of a wonderful resin jewelry maker that I met at a local fair. Diane Dellamano Brakeley uses actual vintage typewriter keys to make her fabulous bracelets, which made such an impression on me that I had to figure out a way to make my own. The trick is locating bezels that imitate the appearance of typewriter keys.

materials

ICE resin

8 15mm oxidized bezels (vintagejewelrysupplies.com)

Typewriter letter collage sheet (rubbernation.com)

10mm link bracelet blank (with 15mm rings), antique silver finish (Rings & Things)

Glossy photo paper

Mod Podge découpage medium

Zap-A-Gap glue

Black permanent marker

Small paintbrush

basic resin supplies

Calibrated mixing cups, craft sticks, toothpicks, straight pin, wax paper, lamp for curing

tools

Computer and printer, sharp craft scissors, ½" (13mm) circle cutter

Finished length:
7" (18cm)

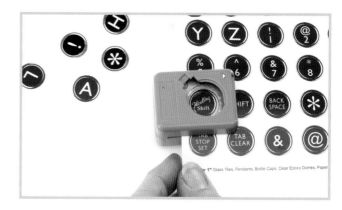

1 Print off the letter sheet, adjusting the print image size so that the letters and symbols fit inside the bezels. (I used the double 5" × 7" [13cm × 18cm] printer setting.) Let the inkjet-printed images dry overnight. Then circle-punch the desired letters, trimming as needed to fit the bezels.

2 Coat both sides of the cut-out letters and symbols with 3 coats of Mod Podge. Apply black permanent marker to the edges of the cut paper if needed, and seal with another coat.

3 Brush Mod Podge inside each bezel and press the coated letters or symbols into the bezels.

4 Use a paintbrush handle to help press the coated pieces into each bezel and release the excess Mod Podge out from under the pieces. Seal the top and edges of each placed circle with another coat of Mod Podge.

5 Mix the resin (see page 11 for preparation) and pour it into each bezel. Make sure the resin in each bezel is level, applying more where you spot any indentation. Let this cure under the lamp for 24 hours.

6 Glue the center back of each bezel to a disk on the bracelet blank.

SAVE THOSE SYMBOLS

This technique lends itself to personalization. Short names or initials are ideal to place in the center of the bracelet. Don't discard the vintage shift symbols and exclamation marks; use them as comical filler on either side of your message.

LITTLE BIRD TOLD ME EARRINGS

A pair of resin bird earrings caught my eye recently, and once I saw them, I knew I wanted to try to re-create them. The trick was to find small earring bezels and a simple graphic that would still read clearly when reduced. Luckily I found both and am pleased with the deeply domed resin tops. This is a pair of earrings that I'd be comfortable wearing almost every day.

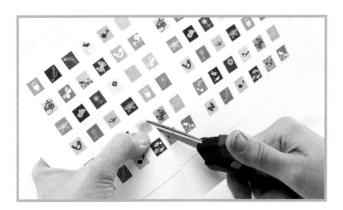

1 First, select your images. I chose a Scrabble tile sheet from Sparrow Graphics featuring simple linear images that would reduce well. I printed the sheet as a pair of 4″ × 6″ (10 cm × 15 cm) photographs. Let the ink dry overnight.

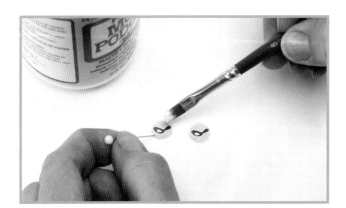

2 If you can't find a circle cutter to fit the bezel size, cut a paper template. Place it over the part of the image you want to feature, then cut out the image. Test-fit the cut image to ensure it will fit inside the bezel. Cut 2 images, one for each earring.

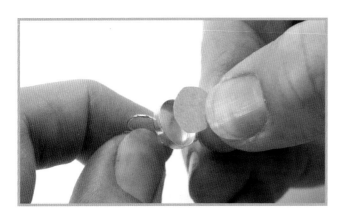

3 Coat the front and back of the bird images with 3 coats of Mod Podge, drying between coats. A straight pin will help hold the small pieces in place as you coat.

materials

ICE resin

Small bird images (etsy.com/shop/sparrowgraphic)

Lever-back 12mm circle earring bezels
(Rings & Things)

2 4mm glass pearl beads

2 silver-ball head pins

Glossy photo paper

Mod Podge découpage medium

Floral foam block

Small paintbrush

basic resin supplies

Calibrated mixing cups, craft sticks, toothpicks, straight pin, wax paper, lamp for curing

tools

Computer and printer, sharp craft scissors, round-nose pliers, needle-nose pliers, flush cutters, blunt wooden stick

Finished dangle length:
1″ (25mm)

tip Tracing around the outside of a bezel to create a template for the inside adds a scant millimeter that will throw off the fit. It's virtually impossible to trace the inside of the bezel, so trim the outer-traced template until it fits inside. If it gets stuck in the bezel, use a straight pin to help pop it out.

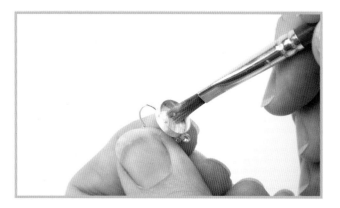

4 Brush Mod Podge inside each bezel.

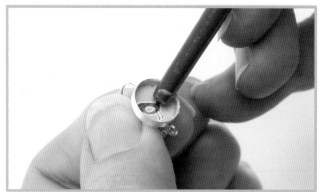

5 Press a bird image into each bezel, using a paintbrush handle to position the bird and release excess Mod Podge out from under each image.

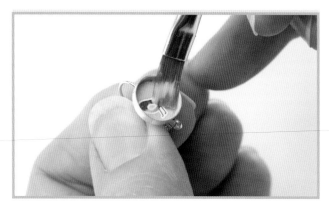

6 Seal the top and edges of each bird image. Let this dry and then recoat with more Mod Podge.

7 Press the lever-back into the floral foam so that the bezel is level.

8 Mix the resin (see page 11 for preparation) and drop it into each bezel with a toothpick. Make sure the resin is level with the top of the bezel. Let it cure under the lamp for 24 hours.

9 With the toothpick, apply a second coat of resin to dome the tops.

10 Slide a pearl bead onto each head pin, and shape the wire around the end of your round-nose pliers. Hook the wire through the ring below the bezel, then wrap the wire end around the base of the loop and trim the excess wire (see *Making a wrapped loop at the end of a head pin* on page 19).

11 Squeeze the wire flat/flush to prevent catching. Push the trimmed wire flat against the last wrap using your needle-nose pliers.

MADE FOR MULTIPLES

Little bezels such as these earrings require such a small amount of resin that it makes sense to pour several pairs at a time. Cut out all the images, seal them, and line them up for pouring. The perfect everyday earrings, you'll want them in an assortment of colors and designs, and your friends will love getting them as gifts.

GOING POSTAL BRACELET

Have you ever taken a moment to really look at the stamps you're placing on your mail? Every stamp is a miniature piece of richly detailed art. Susan Lenart Kazmer's Industrial Chic line features a bezel bracelet blank with rectangular frames that are perfect for holding stamps. I couldn't resist this adorable set of dog stamps and charms.

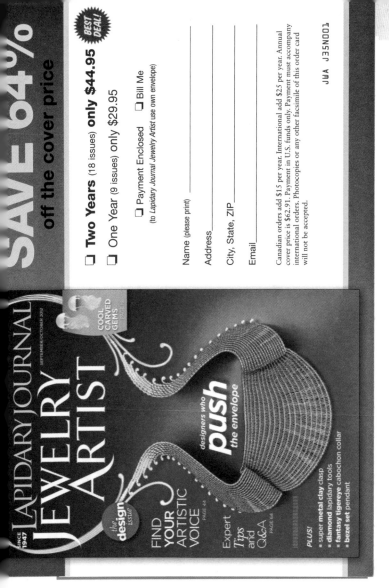

materials

ICE resin

Rectangle bracelet blank (Industrial Chic by Susan Lenart Kazmer)

Assorted postage stamps (dog theme)

4 dog charms

Bead assortment:
3 turquoise 4mm round
3 white 8mm glass
3 bronze 8mm faceted
2 green 7mm
1 green 8mm

4 oval ¼" × ⅜" (7mm x 9mm) jump rings

12 head pins

Mod Podge découpage medium

Small paintbrush

basic resin supplies

Calibrated mixing cups, craft sticks, toothpicks, straight pin, wax paper, lamp for curing, heat gun

tools

Sharp craft scissors, needle-nose pliers, flush cutters

Finished length:
8" (20cm)

2   Select which stamps you want to use in the bracelet bezels. Carefully place the paper template over the portion of the stamp you want to feature, using it as your guide to cut away the unwanted area of the stamp.

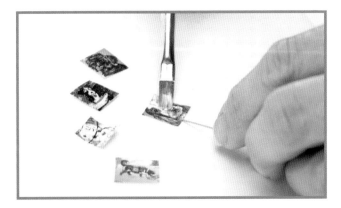

3   Coat the stamp pieces (front and back) with 3 coats of Mod Podge, drying between coats.

4 Brush Mod Podge inside the bezels, then press the coated pieces into them. Use a paintbrush handle to help you position the stamps and release excess Mod Podge out from under them. Seal the top and sides of each stamp with 2 coats of Mod Podge, drying between coats.

5 Mix the resin (see page 11 for preparation) and pour it into each bezel, using a toothpick to spread it to the corners. Make sure the resin is level with the top of the bezels. Check that every bezel is full, and, if necessary, apply more resin to fill indentations. Let it cure under the lamp for 24 hours.

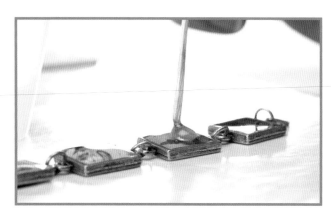

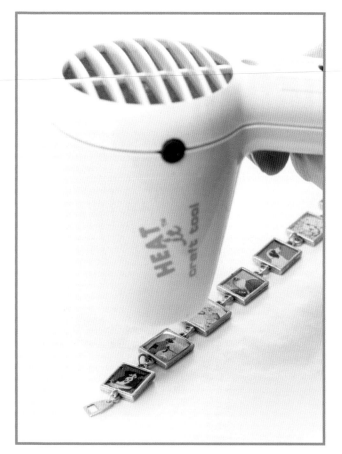

6 With a toothpick, apply a second coat of resin to dome the tops.

7 To help speed curing, use a heat gun at a low temperature.

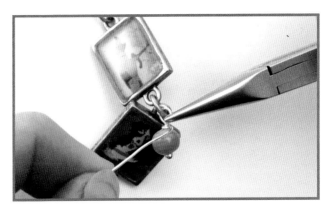

9 Create wrapped-loop beaded dangles, hooking each dangle onto the bracelet (see *Making a wrapped loop at the end of a head pin* on page 19). Attach 2 dangles per bracelet link.

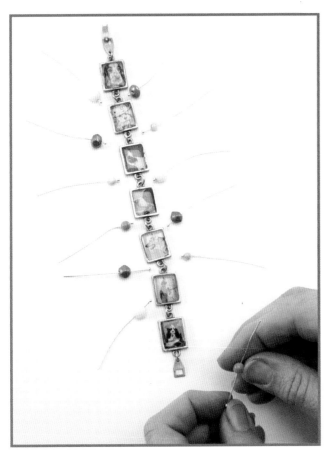

8 Determine the layout of the charms. Then thread beads onto head pins and arrange their order as desired.

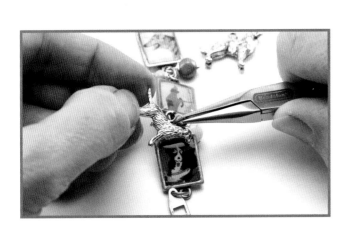

10 Using your needle-nose pliers, thread a charm onto a jump ring (see *Opening and closing a jump ring* on page 19).

11 Attach the charms to the connectors on the bracelet.

PLAY WITH THEMES YOU LOVE

Find a theme that excites you as you collect stamps for this project. Birds have been featured on stamps for ages; I had a nice assortment of images to choose from for this version. Heart stamps and charms would be easy to find for a "love" theme.

HOLIDAY BLING PENDANT

Don't be limited by purchased bezels! 'Tis the season to roll out a piece of clay and make your own. Rhinestones and wire will blend them with chain and vintage jewelry pieces. The magic of UV resin will instantly dome your holiday image.

materials

Lisa Pavelka Magic-Glos UV resin

Pearl polymer clay (Premo! Sculpey Accents)

Holiday collage sheet (ARTchix Studio)

$^{13}/_{16}$" (21mm) ornate round metal bezel (to imprint into the clay) (Vintaj)

8 4mm Swarovski rhinestones

2 velvet ribbons, 11½" × ¼" (29cm × 6mm)

4" (10cm) and 6" (15cm) chains

Vintage rhinestone earring and brooches

3 5mm jump rings

Lobster clasp

20-gauge and 24-gauge black wire

Acrylic paint: silver metallic

Small paintbrush

Clear packing tape

Baking tile

tools & equipment

Craft oven (or a toaster oven used only for baking polymer clay), baking tile, Lisa Pavelka's UV Resin Curing Light, $^{13}/_{16}$" (20mm) circle cutter, sharp craft scissors, bent pliers, round-nose pliers, bent-nose pliers, flush cutters, bent wire finding

Finished length:
31½" (80cm) plus 3" (8cm) pendant (includes flower cluster and dangle)

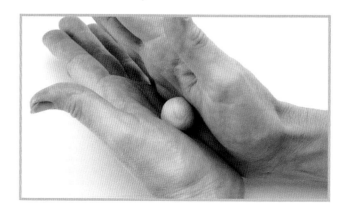

1 Condition the clay with your fingers and roll it into a ½" (13mm) ball. Place the clay on the baking tile.

2 Press the bezel facedown into the clay to leave an impression. Slowly pull it off the clay.

3 Use flush cutters to cut 2½" (13mm) sections of 20-gauge wire. Fold the center of each wire around round-nose pliers to create a U-shaped hanging loop.

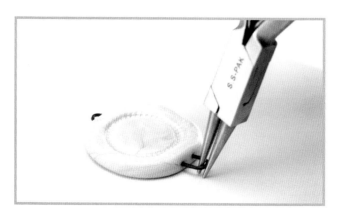

4 Carefully push the wire ends of one loop into the top of the clay bezel, so that the loop extends ¼" (6mm) beyond the clay. Repeat to add the second loop to the base of the bezel.

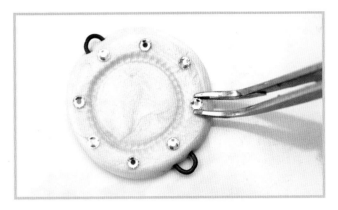

5 Arrange the rhinestones around the edge of the clay. First, position 4 rhinestones at the top, bottom, and each side (like 3, 6, 9 and 12 on a clock face). Then add 4 more rhinestones, one between each of the first 4.

6 Once you're pleased with the placement, press the rhinestones into place.

7 Make impressions in the clay in between each of the rhinestones with a spiraled clasp, stamp, or section of wire. Then bake the bezel according to the polymer clay package instructions.

8 Use the circle cutter to punch out the image you want to use from the collage sheet.

9 Trap the image between 2 layers of clear packing tape.

10 Tightly seal the edges of the image and then cut the image area out of the tape. Be sure to leave a small strip of sealed tape around the outside edge, to prevent the resin from seeping in and spoiling your image.

11 Add a layer of UV resin to the bezel where the image will go.

12 Place the image on the bezel and coat it with a layer of UV resin.

tip *Heat makes bubbles rise to the top and pop. However, don't use this popping technique with any resin except for UV resin.*

13 Cure the resin under the UV light for 5 to 15 minutes. If necessary, apply another coat and place it under the light again.

14 Brush metallic paint into the impressions and quickly wipe away the excess, for just a hint of metallic. Then brush paint onto the raised areas.

16 Loop ribbon ends through the top of the flower cluster. Use a 2" (5cm) long section of 24-gauge wire to wrap the ribbon end to the ribbon length, trapping the flower section in the loop. Trim the wire ends.

15 Glam up your pendant bezel with salvaged costume jewelry components. Use jump rings to attach a crystal dangle to the bottom wire loop and a flower cluster to the top wire (see *Opening and closing a jump ring* on page 19).

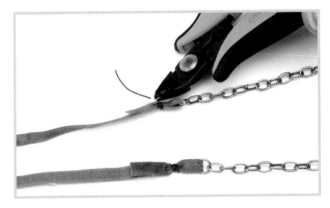

17 Use the same wire-wrapping technique to attach a chain to the end of each ribbon end. Clip the excess wire.

18 Attach a lobster clasp.

VINTAGE TOUCHES ADD UNIQUENESS

Pairing homemade clay bezels with vintage jewelry parts adds to their preciousness. Detour through church and yard sales to collect costume jewelry pieces. Single clip-on earrings, broken or tangled chains, old watches and rhinestone pins can all be disassembled with wire cutters and their components integrated into new creations.

TIMELESS STEAMPUNK PENDANT

Sections of copper pipe make fabulous, deep do-it-yourself bezels. Watch faces are about the same size as small pipes and make great backings for the bezel—but you could easily use images instead. There's plenty of room in these homemade bezels to accommodate charms, rhinestones and watch parts. Don't get stuck in a rut by working with just one metal color; incorporate silver and bronze to add interest to your creations.

materials

ICE resin

1" (25mm) copper pipe

18-gauge copper wire

23" (64cm) copper link chain

Old watch face, backing, springs and watch parts

Moon charm (Blue Moon Beads)

6mm Swarovski crystal bead

Head pin

7mm spring ring clasp

6mm split ring

Zap-A-Gap glue

Clear packing tape

basic resin supplies

Calibrated mixing cups, craft sticks, toothpicks, straight pin, wax paper, lamp for curing

tools

Sharp craft scissors, round-nose pliers, needle-nose pliers, tweezers, flush cutters, pipe cutter, drill with ⅛" (3mm) bit

Finished length:
23" (58cm) plus 1¼" (32mm) pendant

1 Clamp the pipe cutter onto the pipe and crank it around the pipe according to the pipe packaging instructions. It works similar to a can opener, making a straight cut around one section and scoring the pipe until it breaks.

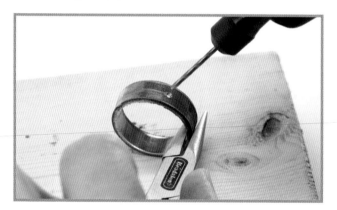

2 Drill a ⅛" (3mm) hole centered on one side of the pipe section. The pipe will get hot as you drill, so be sure to hold it with a clamp or pliers.

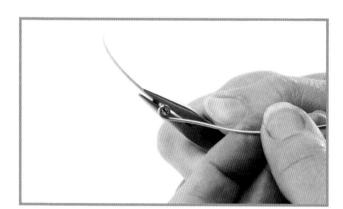

3 Pull out 2" to 3" (5cm to 8cm) of copper wire and bend it at a 90-degree angle using your chain-nose pliers. Spiral the wire around the bend, which should be in the center of the spiral.

4 Push the wire end through the hole so that the spiral rests inside the pipe.

5 Shape the wire into a loop around your needle-nose pliers. Then wrap the wire end around the base of the loop all the way down so that the last rotation lays flat against the pipe (see *Making a wrapped loop at the end of a head pin* on page 19).

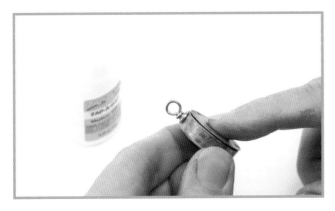

6 Decide whether you want to back your bezel with a watch face or leave it clear. If you opt for the watch face, glue the edges to the base of the pipe.

7 Apply clear packing tape against the back of the watch face and up the sides of the bezel to stop any resin from leaking out around the connection. (You need a nice, tight seal; otherwise, you'll find yourself cutting away cured resin later.)

8 Prepare the pieces that will float in the resin. Here, I am cutting the hanger off a charm.

9 Mix the resin (see page 11 for preparation). Fill the bezel to just under the rim.

10 Use tweezers to place watch parts into the resin. Fill the bezel to the rim with resin and then let it cure under the lamp for 24 hours.

11 Pour a second coat to dome the top. Let this cure for 24 hours.

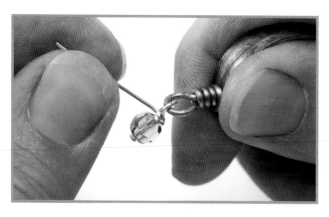

12 String a crystal bead onto the head pin. Loop it through the pendant hanger and wrap the loop (see *Making a wrapped loop at the end of a head pin* on page 19).

13 Add the chain and attach the clasp (see *Opening and closing a jump ring* on page 19).

 tip

Clean your created resin piece no later than 24 hours after finishing the project. It's easier to remove freshly cured overspills the next day. If you wait a few days, the resin will have fully bonded to the bezel and will be harder to peel off.

STEAMPUNK ELEMENTS

Steampunk is the wondrous blend of mechanics, animals and imagination. Utilize all of these elements to make captivating pendants. Don't forget a touch of bling; rhinestones and crystal beads make these creations sparkle.

STAR OF THE SEA NECKLACE

This necklace is inspired by the lovely jewelry made by my friend Julie Brown-Zinchuk while she was living in Higgins Beach in Maine. Her creations helped me realize that most of my designs at the time involved embedding items in resin. These tiny beach treasures are too precious, however, to embed, so instead they are brushed with resin. The shiny cured pieces are framed with Julie's signature pairings of brass filigree and shell buttons.

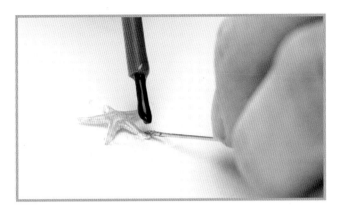

1 Mix the resin (see page 12 for preparation) and brush it onto the front and back of the starfish. Remove any excess and let it cure for 24 hours.

materials

Little Windows resin

Tiny starfish

1⅛" (29mm) shell button

23mm brass circle (Vintaj)

3mm Swarovski rhinestone

Ribbon, 21" × ½" (53cm × 12mm)

Bail, opening 4mm (Rings & Things)

Fold-over crimps

Figure-eight and hook clasp (Vintaj)

Zap-A-Gap glue

Disposable paintbrush

basic resin supplies

Calibrated mixing cups, craft sticks, wax paper, lamp for curing

tools

Needle-nose pliers

Finished length:
20½" (52cm) plus 1⅛" (29mm) pendant

2 Glue the inner brass disk to the button.

3 Glue the starfish to the disk.

4 Glue a tiny rhinestone to the center of the starfish. Let the glue dry.

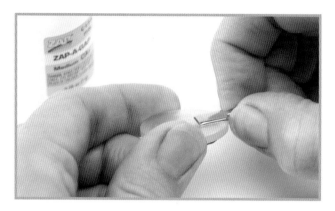

5 Glue the bail to the back of the button.

6 String a ribbon through the bail.

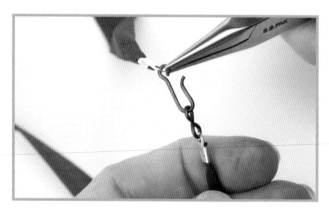

7 Fold crimps over the ribbon ends (see *Folding over crimps* on page 20). Hook on a clasp.

tip

This technique is an ideal way to protect delicate treasures such as sand dollars. When preserving miniature sea urchins, it's important to fill the hollow inside to prevent the piece from crushing flat. This requires two separate resin applications: one to fill the inside and another to coat the outside.

CHEEKY DOUBLE-SIDED EARRINGS

These quick and clever earrings flip to change your mood. Funky little ARTchix images are full of spunky creative messages that are perfect for this project, and the resin sits beautifully on top of the photo paper you'll print them on, making a sealing coat unnecessary. The scalloped silver tape is just for decoration; you can easily skip it and leave the edges plain.

materials

Little Windows resin

Little Windows resin tray

Mini Art Bubbles collage sheet (ARTchix Studio)

Glossy photo paper

2 4mm jump rings

2 eye pins

2 earwires

Double-sided tape

¼" (6mm) silver metal adhesive tape

Zap-A-Gap glue

basic resin supplies

Calibrated mixing cups, craft sticks, stirring stick
(or toothpicks), straight pin, wax paper, lamp for curing

tools

Computer and printer, ⅝" (16mm) circle cutter,
scalloped decorative scissors, sharp craft scissors,
bent-nose pliers, burnishing tool (optional)

Finished dangle length:
½" (12mm)

1 Print off the collage sheet on glossy photo paper and let the ink dry overnight. Punch the desired images out of the sheet (2 for each earring). Set up the paper circles on the Little Windows tray.

2 Mix the resin (see page 12 for preparation) and drop it onto the center of each dot. It should naturally spread to the edges of the paper. If not, use the edge of the stirring tool to encourage it to spread out. Let the resin cure under the lamp for 24 hours.

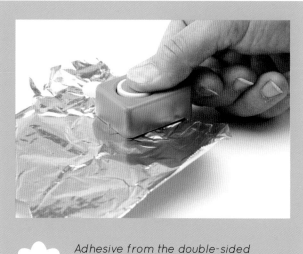

 tip *Adhesive from the double-sided tape can gum up your circle cutter. Sharpen your cutter by punching out a circle from aluminum foil.*

3 Pair the cured pieces together and punch a circle out of the double-sided tape.

4 Remove one side of the backing and press the tape to the back of one circle.

5 Press the eye pin into the adhesive, and add a drop of Zap-A-Gap glue.

6 Press the second side on, making sure the image on each side is right-side up. Repeat the process with the other pair of images.

7 Wrap the metal tape around the outside of the circle to determine the length needed (overlapping by a couple of millimeters) and cut it off the roll.

8 Use scalloped scissors to decoratively trim either side of the tape.

9 Remove the tape's backing and, starting and ending at the eye pin, wrap the center of the tape along the seam of the 2 pieces. Trim away any overlapping tape.

10 Use a craft stick or burnishing tool to smooth the scallops against the resin surface.

11 Thread each earring with a jump ring (see *Opening and closing a jump ring* on page 19) and connect to an earwire.

RESIN PAPER EARRINGS

Resin paper is an exciting concept that couldn't be easier to try. Simply coat both sides of a paper design with ICE resin, then trap the paper between plastic bags while it cures. The resulting dried paper is lightweight and magnificently translucent. Protected by cured resin, it is incredibly easy to cut and frame in wire hoops, making it ideal for crafting customized earrings.

materials

ICE resin

Bird collage sheet (Nunn Design)

2 8mm Swarovski crystal beads

20-gauge black wire

2 earwires

2 head pins

Zap-A-Gap glue

Foam paintbrush

Trash bag

Packing tape

Heavy book

basic resin supplies

Calibrated mixing cups, craft sticks

tools

$^{13}/_{16}$" (20mm) circle cutter, sharp craft scissors, ring
mandrel, round-nose pliers, needle-nose pliers, flush
cutters, jeweler's hammer, metal block

Finished dangle length:
1" (25mm)

1 Select and cut 2 sections of the collage sheet
that you want to feature in your earrings.

2 Cut open a trash bag, then stretch and tape it
flat to your work surface. (You'll need a second
piece to cover the paper, too.) Mix a small amount of
resin (see page 11 for preparation) and use the foam
brush to coat both sides of the paper.

3 Place the coated paper on the plastic, cover it
with the second piece of plastic, and smooth
out the wrinkles. Then weight it with a book to keep
it flat. Let it dry overnight.

4 Carefully peel up the dried resin paper.

5 Insert the dried resin paper into the circle cutter and punch out 2 circles.

6 Prepare the 20-gauge wire for the hoops by hammering it flat on your metal block.

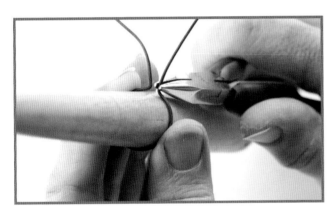

7 Determine what spot on the ring mandrel corresponds to the size of the punched paper pieces, then wrap the flattened wire around this spot. Use needle-nose pliers to bend the wire up at a 90-degree angle where the wires meet.

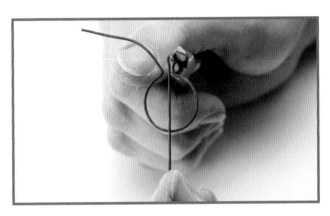

8 Shape one wire end into a loop around your round-nose pliers.

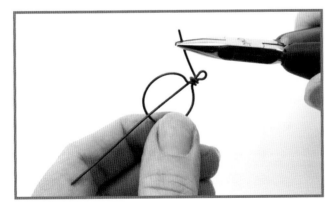

9 While grasping the loop in your chain-nose pliers, wrap the other wire around the base of the loop and then trim away the end. Make a second hoop for the other earring.

10 Working with one hoop at a time, apply glue to the back of the hoop and then carefully place the paper image-side up under the hoop.

11 String a crystal bead onto the head pin and shape the end into a loop around your round-nose pliers, then trim the wire.

12 Hook the wire into the top of the hoop, and then close the loop. Repeat for the second earring.

13 Hook an earwire to the top of each wire hoop.

tip

While you're spreading out plastic bags and mixing resin, it makes sense to coat multiple pieces of paper. Some of my favorite earrings use vintage sheet music and instructional piano books discovered in our garage sale piano bench.

SQUARE IT UP

The beauty of custom wire frames is that you can create a frame to fit around any image or shape. Form rectangular frames by pinching corners in the wire with chain-nose pliers. Bring the wire ends together at the center top of the frame and create a wrapped hanging loop.

EMBEDDED SHELL PENDANT

Any beachcomber recognizes the beauty of wet shells being washed ashore. Like water, resin deepens the color and heightens the natural beauty of shells. Suspending them in resin perfectly preserves your ocean collectibles in the lovely state they were found in.

materials

ICE resin

Rectangular mold (in the assorted Castin' Craft mold tray)

Contrasting shells (orange snail, blue mussels)

16" (41cm) serpentine necklace (Blue Moon Beads)

Large bail, 7mm opening (Rings & Things)

Large lobster clasp

Mold release spray

Sandpaper in 300, 400 & 600 grit

Zap-A-Gap glue

Carnauba car wax

Old cloth towels

Zippered plastic bag

basic resin supplies

Calibrated mixing cups, craft sticks, toothpicks, straight pin, wax paper, lamp for curing

tools

Sharp craft scissors, bent tweezers, rubber mallet

Finished length:
16" (41cm) plus 1½" (38mm) pendant

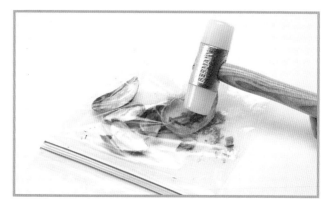

1 Spray mold release into the rectangular mold and let it dry. Put the mussel shells inside a zippered plastic bag and then crush them with the rubber mallet.

2 Pour a ¼" (6mm) of prepared resin (see page 11 for preparation) into the mold.

3 Tilt the tray to help release the bubbles, then lay the tray flat and let the resin set up for 5 minutes.

4 Position the orange shell facedown in the mold with bent tweezers.

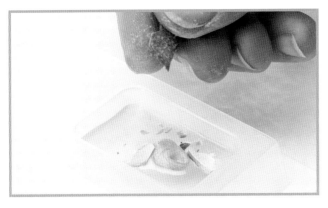

5 Sprinkle the crushed mussel shell pieces around the orange shell.

6 Fill the rest of the mold with resin.

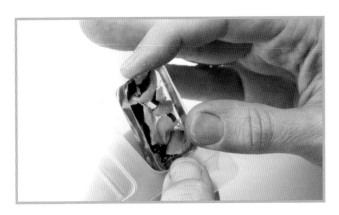

7 Let the resin cure under the lamp for 24 hours, then pop it out of the mold.

8 Trim and sand the edges of the cured resin, starting with 300-grit sandpaper, continuing with 400-grit, and finishing with 600-grit (see *Finishing techniques* on page 17). Rinse the sanded piece with water.

9 Coat the sanded resin with car wax using a towel. Then rub off the wax with a clean towel.

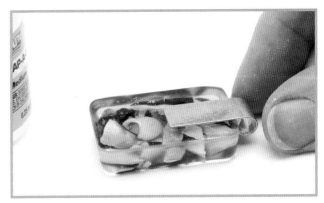

10 Glue the bail to the back.

CREDIT ON ICE BANGLES

Cutting up credit cards has never been so much fun! Trap colorful pieces of old or expired gift and credit cards in crystal-clear resin, poured into one of three bangle mold sizes (small, medium or large). This interest-free jewelry is sure to be a conversation starter.

1 Spray mold release into the bangle mold and let it dry. Then cut up old credit and gift cards.

materials
Castin' Craft resin
3¼" (8cm) bangle mold (Rings & Things)
Old credit and gift cards
Mold release spray
Sandpaper in 300, 400 & 600 grit
Disposable paintbrush

basic resin supplies
Nitrile gloves, calibrated mixing cups, craft sticks, toothpicks, straight pin, wax paper, lamp for curing

tools
Sharp craft scissors

Finished size:
3¼" (8cm) bangle

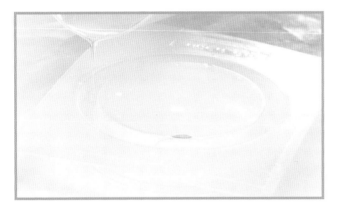

2 Pour prepared resin (see page 10 for preparation) into the mold until it is three-quarters of the way full (enough resin for the card pieces to stand upright when placed). *NOTE:* Be sure to wear your gloves when handling this type of resin.

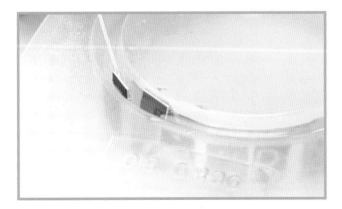

3 Using a toothpick, position the cut-up card pieces in the resin (not all in one direction, or overlapping).

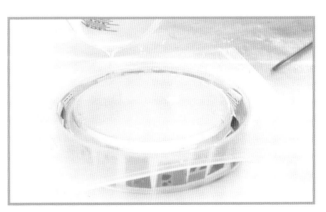

4 Fill the rest of the bangle mold with resin.

5 The card pieces will likely shift a bit with the last pour. Reposition them as needed with a toothpick. Let the bangle cure under the lamp for 24 hours (it may take slightly longer, due to the large amount of resin). As the resin cures, you may find the credit card pieces floating upward. If you don't encounter any resistance (surface tension), you can push the pieces back down with a toothpick. You don't want those pieces poking up (and poking you!) once the resin has dried.

6 Once the bangle has cured, put it in the freezer for a few minutes to help it pop out of the mold easily.

7 Sand the bangle, starting with 300-grit sandpaper, continuing with 400-grit, and finishing with 600-grit.

tip

Bangle molds come in assorted sizes and thicknesses. There is a substantial weight difference between the largest and smallest bracelets. Choose whichever will be the most comfortable for you to wear. Once you've invested in a bracelet mold, experiment with trapping a variety of items in the resin: colored wires, beads, dried flowers.

8 Apply a topcoat of resin for a crystal-clear finish (see *Finishing techniques* on page 17).

TRANSPARENT PENDANT

Nothing shows off the icelike clarity of resin like trapping a transparent image in it. I chose to use gorgeous photos taken by a dear college friend of mine, Mary Johanna Brown, who runs a graphic design firm in New Hampshire. Simply shrink your image to 1" (25mm) in size and print it on a transparency sheet. I got much better results by taking the images to a print shop that used a toner printer rather than an inkjet.

materials

ICE resin

1¼" (32mm) square mold (Castin' Craft mold tray)

Clear transparency or shrink plastic sheet

Photo (image by Mary Johanna Brown)

18" (46cm) cable wire necklace with clasp
(Rings & Things)

20-gauge silver-plated copper wire

Mold release spray

basic resin supplies

Calibrated mixing cups, craft sticks, toothpicks,
straight pin, wax paper, lamp for curing

tools

Sharp craft scissors, drill with ⅛" (3mm) bit, round-nose
pliers, wire cutters, low-temperature heat gun

Finished length:
18" (46cm) plus 1¼" (32mm) pendant

1 Select a sharp-focus image with rich color, reduce it to 1" (25mm) in size, and print it on a clear transparency or shrink plastic sheet. (I got the best results from a laser printer, which uses toner cartridges; my inkjet printer created a bumpy appearance.) Spray mold release into the square mold and let it dry. Cut the image to the border.

2 Mix the resin (see page 11 for preparation) and pour a small amount into the mold.

3 Tilt the mold so that the resin coats the entire bottom of the mold.

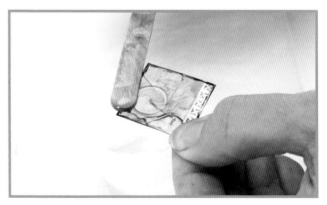

4 Use a craft stick to coat the shrunken image with resin.

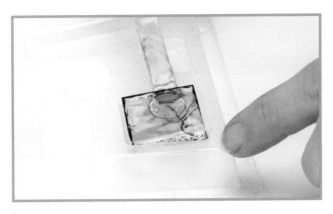

5 Gently set the image onto the mold. Check for any trapped air bubbles; apply light pressure to the back of the image to release them. Hit it with a low-temperature heat gun to disperse surface bubbles.

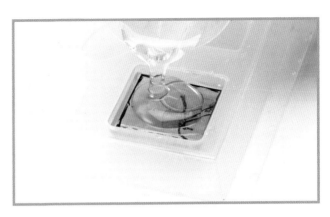

6 Pour resin over the image to fill the mold. Let the resin fully cure under the lamp for 24 hours.

7 Pop the cured resin out of the mold.

8 Trim around the piece as needed with the scissors to remove any excess resin.

9 Drill a ⅛" (3mm) hole into the center top of the cured piece (see *Drilling cured pieces* on page 17).

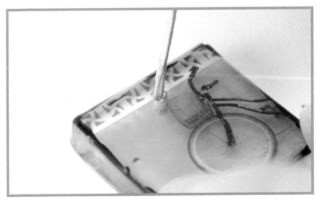

10 Using a toothpick, coat the inside of the hole with resin to make it clear again, and let it dry (see *Finishing techniques* on page 17).

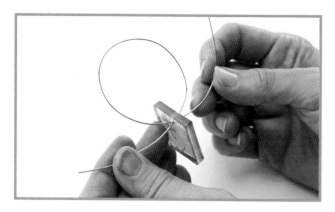

11 To create the hanger for the pendant, cut an 11½" (29cm) length of the 20-gauge wire and string it through the hole as shown.

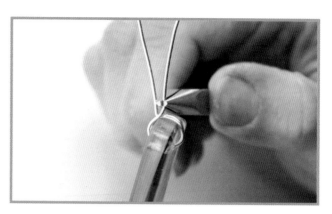

12 Bend up one of the wires at a 90-degree angle at the top of the pendant, using chain-nose pliers.

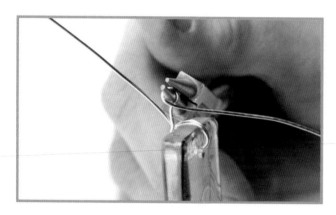

13 Using your round-nose pliers, wrap the bent wire into a loop, leaving enough room below the loop for wrapping the wire 4 times.

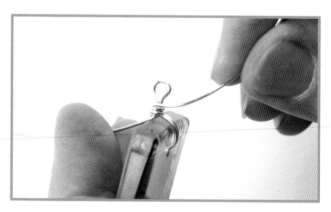

14 Wrap the wire under the loop 4 times.

15 Trim the ends of the wire.

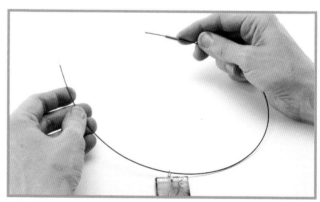

16 String the pendant onto a purchased cable wire necklace.

CLEARLY BEAUTIFUL COLOR

This pendant showcases another Mary Jo Brown photograph. The saturated color and bright blue background make an eye-catching focal point. If you're having a hard time finding new images for your jewelry, consider searching through old slides. You might find a simple image that will show up clearly in a pendant.

STAMPED AND MAGNIFIED PENDANT

The distortion of the image seen through the resin in this pendant is a play on looking through a camera lens. The deep cabochon mold was the perfect fit for the fun vintage camera images I found. And, if you've never tried it before, you'll be amazed at how easy it is to stamp letters and words onto metal tags. I couldn't resist stamping "smile" on mine!

1 Print off the collage sheet as a pair of 5" × 7" (13cm × 18cm) images on an 8½" × 11" (22cm × 28cm) sheet of glossy photo paper (no need to let them dry, as they will be sealed in tape). This should ensure that you have a nice selection of small images to choose from. Cut out the camera you want, removing all the white edges.

materials

ICE resin

20mm square cabochon molds (Rings & Things)

Vintage camera collage sheet (etsy.com/shop/midnightbluart)

30mm × 17mm metal rectangular tag

7mm brass jump ring

23" (58cm) ball-and-chain necklace

Letter stamps

Glossy photo paper

Mold release spray

Clear packing tape

Zap-A-Gap glue

basic resin supplies

Calibrated mixing cups, craft sticks, toothpicks, straight pin, wax paper, lamp for curing

tools

Computer and printer, sharp craft scissors, rubber mallet, bench block, chain-nose pliers, bent-nose pliers (optional)

Finished length:
23" (58cm) plus 1½" (4cm) pendant

2 Test-fit the camera image in the cabochon mold. Leaving a little space around the image will help any post-pour air bubbles to escape.

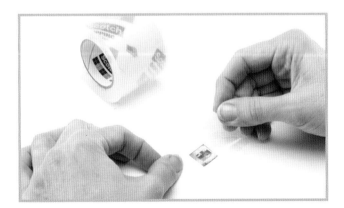

3 Sandwich the image between 2 layers of clear packing tape.

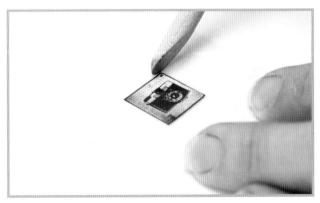

4 Seal the edges with a craft stick (or you could use a burnisher or bone folder).

5 Trim away the excess tape (not too close, or else you'll break the seal).

6 Spray mold release into the cabochon mold and let it dry.

7 Mix the resin (see page 11 for preparation) and pour enough into the cabochon mold to completely fill it.

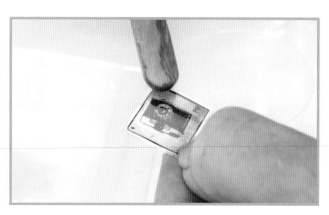

8 Apply resin to both sides of the image.

9 Place the coated image facedown over the mold. Carefully pick up the mold and look at it from underneath to check for air bubbles. (If you discover bubbles, see *Bubble control* on pages 14–15.) Let the piece cure under the lamp for 24 hours.

10 Working over a bench block, stamp one letter at a time along the bottom of the metal tag, making sure that each is facing the right direction and is aligned with the edge, and applying even pressure with the mallet. Don't let the stamp shift, or it will form a second stamp on the tag.

11 Remove the cured cabochon from the mold.

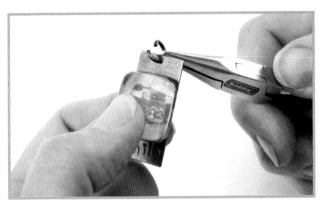

12 Trim the edges with scissors, but don't sand them. Sanding will actually opaque (or cloud) the resin, which you don't want because it's just getting glued to the metal back.

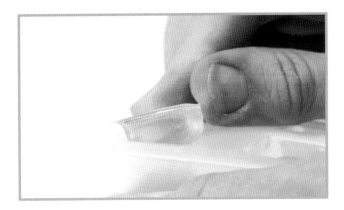

13 Use Zap-A-Gap glue to attach the cabochon to the metal tag. Press it firmly onto the metal while letting it dry.

14 Attach a jump ring to the metal tag (see *Opening and closing a jump ring* on page 19).

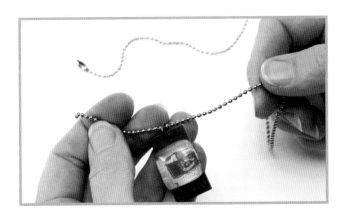

15 String the ball-and-chain necklace through the jump ring.

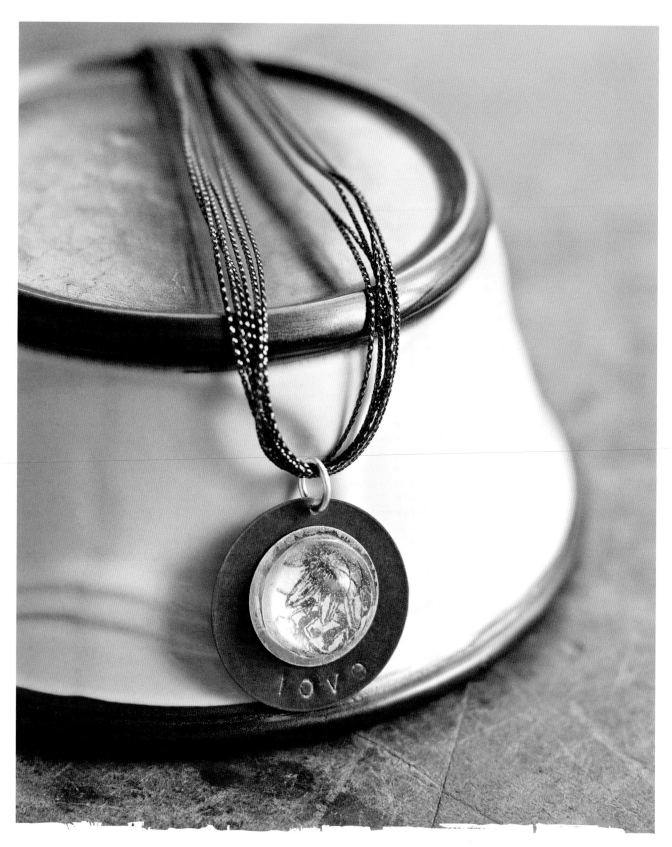

SIMPLE LINES AND COLOR

Midnightbluart (Etsy.com) also has a great collage sheet of natural images in blue and black. The limited two-color palette and simple line drawing enables the image to reduce well and show up under the deep resin magnification.

FAUX SEA GLASS PENDANT

If you love the look of sea glass, you'll be amazed by how easy it is to re-create in resin. Pouring tinted resin into a hoop earring mold makes the circle, and sanding the entire surface of the cured hoop instantly creates a frosted look. Adding a silver hook bail, vintage flower beads, and a touch of sparkle transforms a simple hoop into a stunning pendant.

materials

Castin' Craft resin

Castin' Craft Transparent Dye: Blue, Green

34mm hoop earring mold (Sherri Haab)

25mm long silver metal hook bail (Rings & Things)

18" (46cm) cable wire necklace with clasp
(Rings & Things)

5mm reclaimed rhinestone from vintage jewelry

7mm & 12mm vintage plastic flower beads

Mold release spray

Sandpaper in 300, 400 & 600 grit

Zap-A-Gap glue

basic resin supplies

Nitrile gloves, calibrated mixing cups, craft sticks,
toothpicks, straight pin, wax paper, lamp for curing

tools

Sharp craft scissors

Finished length:
18" (46cm) plus 2" (5cm) pendant (includes bail)

1 Spray mold release into the hoop mold and let it dry. Mix 1 ounce of resin (see page 10 for preparation). To color the resin, add 2 drops of blue and 1 drop of green. *NOTE:* Be sure to wear your gloves when handling this type of resin.

2 Use a craft stick or stirring tool to blend the color into the resin.

tip

Carefully add pigment one drop of color at a time. The only way to lighten darkly pigmented resin is to dilute it with clear resin. Darkening resin is easy—just add drops and mix until you're satisfied with the appearance. The color stays the same as it dries. Sanding the surface will frost it and give it a lighter appearance.

3 Pour the colored resin into the hoop mold (1 ounce will make multiple hoops).

4 Let the hoop cure under the lamp for 24 hours, then pop it out of the mold and trim the edges with scissors.

tip An emery board is an ideal tool for sanding around the inside and outside of the hoop.

5 Sand all sides of the hoop to distress the surface, beginning with 300-grit sandpaper and gradually progressing to 600-grit (see *Sanding* on page 16). Then rinse the piece with water.

6 Hook the hoop onto the bail and use chain-nose pliers to pinch it closed.

7 Arrange 2 plastic flower beads over the flat portion of the metal hook. Once you're happy with the arrangement, glue them in place and add a rhinestone center.

FROSTED DELIGHT

This pendant was created with the larger hoop in the mold tray. You don't need the specialized mold to play with this technique; you can pour the resin into a plain square or circle mold and drill a large hole into the cured resin. The real trick is the sanded finish that creates that frosted appearance.

CUTE AS A BUTTON EARRINGS

Two-part mold putty makes it so easy to create your own reusable resin molds. Grab a selection of your favorite buttons to push into the putty. Simply brush and pour tinted resin into the cured molds, then pop out the resin shapes and incorporate them into jewelry such as these charming flower earrings.

materials

ICE resin

Castin' Craft EasyMold Silicone Putty

Castin' Craft Transparent Dye: Blue

Castin' Craft Opaque Pigment: White

2 ⅝" (16mm) flower buttons

2 4mm bicone crystals

4 eye pins

Earwires

Mold release spray

Zap-A-Gap glue

Sandpaper in 300, 400 & 600 grit

Small paintbrush

basic resin supplies

Nitrile gloves, calibrated mixing cups, craft sticks, toothpicks, wax paper, lamp for curing

tools

Flush cutters, round-nose pliers, drill with ⅛" (3mm) bit

Finished dangle length:
1" (25mm)

1 Follow package instructions and mix together equal parts of purple and white silicone putty. When the colors are completely blended, roll the silicone into a ball.

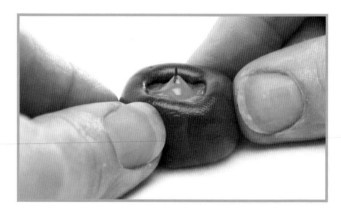

2 Push a flower button facedown into the clay, massaging the clay up around the button. Make a second mold so that when you mix the colored resin, you can pour matching earrings.

3 Let the compound cure for about 25 minutes and then pop out the buttons. Let the molds cure completely for 24 hours, then prepare them with mold release spray and let them dry completely before proceeding.

4 Mix the resin (see page 11 for preparation) and pour a small amount into a separate cup. Tint it with 2 drops of blue dye and 2 drops of white pigment. Mix the color until it's fully blended and then let it rest for 1–2 minutes to let the bubbles dissipate.

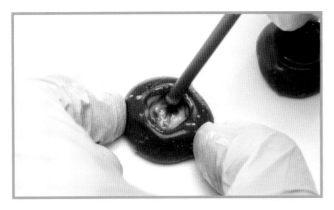

5 Brush resin into all the cracks and crevices in each mold, to prevent bubbles.

6 Once you're certain that all the petals have had resin pushed into them, pour resin to fill both molds. Pick up each mold and tap it on the tabletop to release any trapped air.

7 Let the resin cure overnight under the lamp before popping out the flowers.

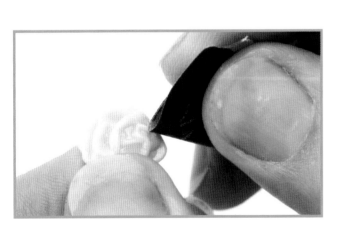

8 Sand away any small bubbles, which usually will appear at the edges.

tip

This was one of my early failed attempts. The resin wasn't brushed into all the petals in the mold before the pouring. The trapped air bubble caused a broken petal.

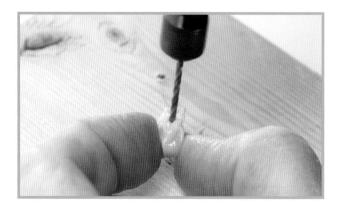

9 Using a ⅛" (3mm) bit, drill a small hole in each flower for the eye pin hanger.

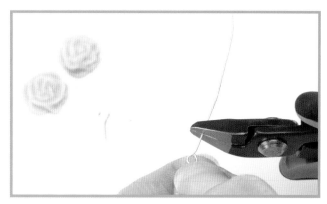

10 Trim the end off of 2 eye pins until the pin end fits into the drilled hole and the eye sits above the flower edge.

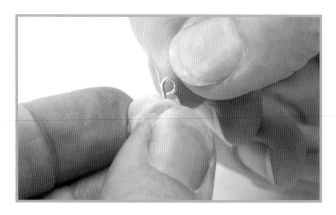

11 Glue an eye pin end into each flower.

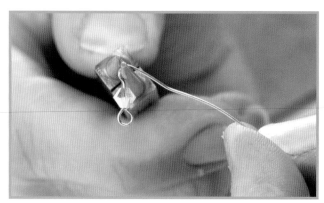

12 Thread a bicone crystal onto each of the other untrimmed eye pins and create a loop using round-nose pliers.

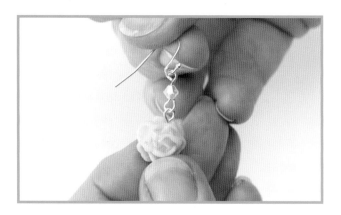

13 Join one end of the crystal connector to the flower and the other to the earwire.

MULTIPLY AND CONQUER

Assemble a variety of buttons, plastic and glass ephemera before rolling out your molds. Like most resin projects, it's best to mix and pour multiple molds at a time. If you end up with a bubble in one, you're guaranteed to have more that are ready to turn into jewelry.

HOOTENANNY BRACELET

Wear your wisdom on your sleeve! Two striking owls are nestled between double strands of colorful stones, beads and brass findings on this lovely bracelet, creating an eye-pleasing blend of natural and manmade materials and nontraditional shapes. The owls' proportions are ideal for mold making.

1 Follow package instructions and mix together equal parts of purple and white silicone putty. When the colors are completely blended, roll the silicone into a ball.

2 Push the owl bead facedown into the clay (the bead shown is two-sided). Let the compound cure for about 25 minutes, then pop out the bead. Create a second mold so that you can pour both owls at the same time. Then let both molds cure completely for 24 hours, coat with mold release spray, and let dry completely before proceeding.

3 Mix the resin (see page 11 for preparation) and pour a small amount into a separate cup. Tint it with 3 drops of amber dye and 1 drop of white pigment.

materials

ICE resin

Castin' Craft Transparent Dye: Amber

Castin' Craft Opaque Pigment: White

Castin' Craft EasyMold Silicone Putty

Two-sided owl bead (Beadin' Path)

4 horn beads in assorted shapes

Round and disk-shape beads (Blue Moon Beads):
9 brass-colored crimp beads
4 7mm round
4 4mm turquoise round
3 14mm × 12mm orange stone oval
3 12mm turquoise disk
3 9mm red stone round
2 10mm wood brown disk

.015 brass stringing wire (Beadalon)

Brass jump rings: 4 small (7mm), 1 large (14mm) (Vintaj)

2 13mm brass figure-eight rings (Vintaj)

1 large brass hook (Vintaj)

Mold release spray

Sandpaper in 300, 400 & 600 grit

Small paintbrush

basic resin supplies

Nitrile gloves, calibrated mixing cups, craft sticks, toothpicks, lamp for curing

tools

Sharp craft scissors, flush cutters, crimping pliers, drill with 1/16" (2mm) bit

Finished length:
7 3/4" (20cm)

4 Mix the color until it's fully blended, and then let it rest for 1–2 minutes to let the bubbles dissipate.

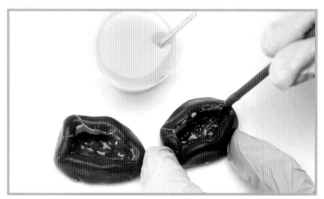

5 Brush resin into all the cracks and crevices in the mold.

6 Once you are sure that all the crevices are filled, pour resin to fill the rest of the mold. Pick up the mold and tap it on the tabletop to release any trapped air.

7 Let the resin cure overnight under the lamp before popping out the owls. Sand away any rough edges on the back of the owls so they'll feel smooth against your skin (see *Sanding* on page 16).

8 Tip each owl on its side and drill a hole at the neck that spans across the inside of the body and comes out the other side of the neck. Make a second hole a ½" (13mm) down from the first.

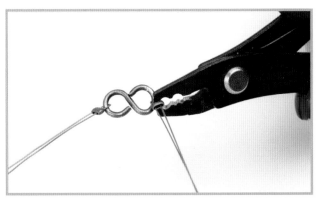

9 Loop a 20" (51cm) strand of stringing wire through one side of the figure-eight ring, pulling it through so the middle of the length sits in the metal loop. String both ends through a crimp bead. Slide the bead down against the figure eight and squeeze the crimp flat.

Repeat the process to connect a double strand to the other side of the figure eight.

10 Begin stringing 1⅜" (35mm) of a random assortment of beads onto each pair of wires.

11 String the top pair of wires through the top hole in the owl, then string the bottom pair through the bottom hole.

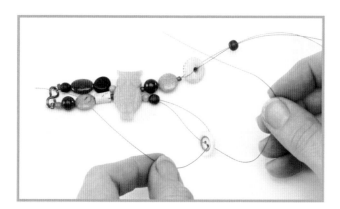

12 To ensure the button and disk beads lay flat, separate the paired wires and thread them in opposite directions through the center hole. One will go from front to back, the other back to front. For the buttons, repeat the process to string the wires through the second hole.

13 String 1¾" (44mm) of more button and disk beads onto each pair of wires, thread on the second owl, then finish the bracelet with 1⅜" (35mm) of beading.

14 String one pair of wires through a crimp bead and loop it through one side of a second figure-eight ring before bringing the ends back through the crimp. Squeeze the crimp closed. Repeat the process to connect the second pair of wires to the other side of the figure-eight ring.

15 Use a pair of small jump rings (see *Opening and closing a jump ring* on page 19) to attach a large ring to one figure-eight ring, and a hook to the other figure-eight ring.

COPYCAT CLOISONNÉ EARRINGS

Traditional cloisonné involves placing powdered enamel onto a metal surface. The colors fuse into an enamel veneer under high heat. My resin version is much easier and doesn't involve the use of a kiln. Katie Hacker's line of Katiedids components (Beadalon) are ideal for this project. They feature deep channels for holding resin, and predrilled holes allow you to shape wire hanging loops before pouring.

materials

ICE resin

Castin' Craft Opaque Pigment: Green, White, Yellow

2 Katiedids rectangles

8 4 mm blue beads

2 head pins

Modern earwires (Beadalon)

2 4mm jump rings

Adhesive tape

basic resin supplies

Nitrile gloves, calibrated mixing cups, craft sticks, toothpicks, emery board, straight pin, wax paper, baby wipes, lamp for curing

tools

Flush cutters, round-nose pliers, needle-nose pliers, bent-nose pliers

Finished dangle length:
¾" (19mm)

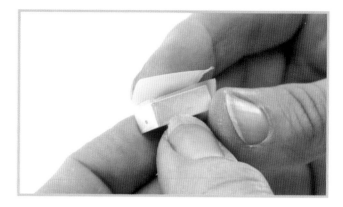

1 Apply adhesive tape to the sides and back of each rectangle component.

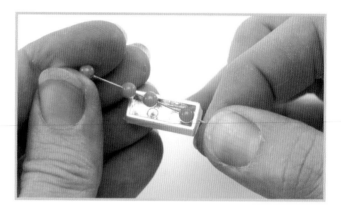

2 Poke a head pin through the hole in the base of each component. String on 4 beads.

3 Bring the wire out the top of each component and wrap it around the round-nose pliers to make a hanging loop. Then wrap the wire end around the base of the loop (see *Making a wrapped loop at the end of a head pin* on page 19).

4 Mix 1 ounce of resin (see page 11 for preparation). Add a drop of each of the green, yellow and white pigments.

5 Stir the solution until it is fully blended, adding additional drops of color as needed to achieve the desired tint.

6 Carefully pour the blended resin into the prepared components. *NOTE:* Although the resin is self-leveling, you can manipulate it with a toothpick to help distribute it evenly.

7 Use a baby wipe to remove resin from the sides of each component and the tops of the beads. Let each piece cure under the lamp for 24 hours.

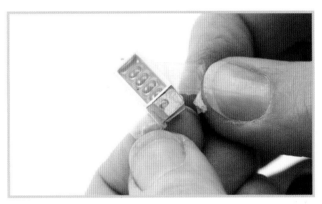

8 Remove the tape and clean off any stray pieces of resin by carefully popping them off with an emery board.

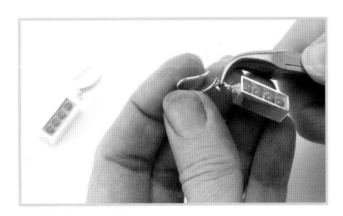

9 Hook the earwires in place with small jump rings and bent-nose pliers (see *Opening and closing a jump ring* on page 19).

CHANGING CHANNELS

Katiedids components with double channels offer two separate sections to fill with color. Instead of shaping a head pin hanger for this pendant, I drilled a hole through both the cured resin and the bezel. Then I looped a hanging jump ring through the opening. Thick leather cord is the perfect weight to counterbalance the hefty pendant.

KEEP-THE-PIECE FABRIC PENDANT

If you're drawn to gorgeous fabric, this project is for you. Trapped in clear resin, this tiny fabric swatch stays shiny and new. A second white pour gives the pendant a luminous backing. An added brass flower and rhinestone center shows off the depth of the pendant.

materials

Little Windows resin

Castin' Craft Opaque Pigment: White

45mm × 17mm rectangle mold (in the assorted Castin' Craft mold tray)

Fabric scraps

15mm brass flower (Vintaj)

3mm Swarovski rhinestone

Bail, 4mm opening

18" (46cm) cable wire necklace with clasp (Industrial Chic by Susan Lenart Kazmer)

Jewelry glue

Mod Podge découpage medium

Mold release spray

Emery board

Small paintbrush

basic resin supplies

Nitrile gloves, calibrated mixing cups, craft sticks, toothpicks, straight pin, wax paper

tools

Sharp craft scissors, bent tweezers

Finished length:
18" (46cm) plus 1¾" (44mm) pendant

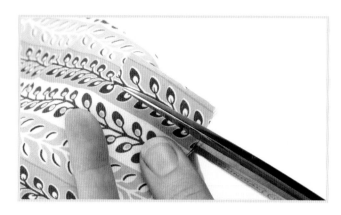

1 Cut the fabric to fit the rectangular mold. Then remove the fabric, spray the mold with mold release, and let it dry.

2 Coat the front and back of the fabric with 3 coats of Mod Podge, drying between coats.

3 Pour ¼" (6mm) of the prepared resin (see page 12 for preparation) into the mold and let it set up for 5 minutes.

4 Use a craft stick to coat the fabric with resin.

5 Lay the coated fabric facedown in the resin, and let the resin cure.

6 Mix a second batch of resin and tint it with 3 drops of white pigment. Then fill up the rest of the mold and let it cure for 24 hours.

7 Pop the cured piece out of the mold, then trim the edges as needed. Sand the edges with an emery board.

8 Glue the bail to the back of the pendant.

9 Glue the flower and rhinestone center to the front of the pendant.

10 String the cable wire necklace with clasp through the bail.

MAKE MANY FROM ONE

A single piece of fabric may yield a number of pendant options. It all depends on which portion of the fabric you choose. To make the best use of your time, prepare several pieces of fabric to fit the different mold shapes and sizes. Pouring multiple pendants at once minimizes resin waste.

BUTTERFLY BEAUTY PENDANT

One of my first serious antique collections was butterfly wing jewelry—gorgeous sections of blue wings trapped under domed glass and soldered in silver. I shudder to think how many blue morpho butterflies met an untimely end for this Victorian trend. If you stumble across one that has died from natural causes, keep it and preserve those beautiful wings in resin.

materials

Little Windows resin

30mm round resin mold (Little Windows)

Castin' Craft Opaque Pigment: Black

Real butterfly wings

Scrapbook paper (DCWV)

Word stickers (Pebbles Inc.)

Silver bail, 4mm opening (Beadalon)

18" (46cm) ball-and-chain necklace

Mod Podge découpage medium

Zap-A-Gap glue

Black permanent marker

Clear packing tape

Sandpaper in 300, 400 & 600 grit

Small paintbrush

basic resin supplies

Nitrile gloves, calibrated mixing cups, craft sticks,
toothpicks, straight pin, wax paper, lamp for curing

tools

Sharp craft scissors, circle cutter (matching the size
of your circle mold)

Finished length:
18" (46cm) plus 1¼" (44mm) pendant

1 Use a circle cutter to punch a circle out of the scrapbook paper.

2 Carefully cut a portion of a butterfly wing to place across part of the circle. (Cut very carefully; butterfly wings are incredibly delicate.)

3 Lift up the wing and brush Mod Podge where it will be placed, and over the top of it. Gently press the wing in place and apply more Mod Podge. Add a word or image sticker to your design and coat it, and finally the entire paper circle, with Mod Podge.

4 Apply permanent marker around the outside edge of the circle (the black edge will help the paper blend into the background). Next apply a coat of Mod Podge to the back of the paper, then add 2 more coats to the front and the back, drying between coats.

5 Mix the resin (see page 12 for preparation). Pour a ¼" (6mm) of resin into the round mold and let it set up for 5 minutes.

6 Use a craft stick to apply a coat of resin to the front and back of the paper circle.

7 Place the paper circle facedown into the mold. Carefully lift the mold and look at it from underneath to make sure no air bubbles have formed under the paper. Let it cure under the lamp for 24 hours.

8 Mix another batch of resin and stir in enough drops of pigment to make it black. If necessary, add 1–2 more drops to ensure the color is opaque. But, be aware that adding too much pigment can affect the drying time.

9 Add the black resin on top of the paper circle in the mold. Make sure you've added enough resin so that the top (the pendant back) is level and flush with the top of the mold. Let it cure under the lamp for 24 hours. Here, I filled a few molds.

10 Pop out the cured piece and then sand the black edges, beginning with 300-grit sandpaper and gradually progressing to 600-grit (see *Sanding* on page 16).

11 Anchor the sanded piece on tape and apply a topcoat of resin (see *Finishing techniques* on page 17).

12 Glue the bail to the back of the pendant.

ON THE EDGE

The black edge and back takes the place of a bezel, giving these pendants a professional finish. Play with different color and wing combinations. As always, it makes sense to plan multiple pendants before mixing the resin.

FOR-THE-BIRDS TRANSFER PENDANT

I was a little skeptical before starting this project, but it had nothing to do with the resin—
I just couldn't understand how the image on the paper could transfer onto the polymer clay.
However, it does work; try it for yourself. White clay brightens the gorgeous birds on the
Becky Nunn collage sheet. A magical coat of Lisa Pavelka's UV resin gives a shiny finish.

materials

Lisa Pavelka Magic-Glos UV resin

White polymer clay (Sculpey)

Bird collage sheet (Nunn Design)

30mm × 25mm brass bezel (Vintaj)

19" (48cm) brass link chain (Vintaj)

4 brass head pins (Vintaj)

1 eye pin

2 6mm jump rings

Brass lobster clasp

4 4mm blue stones

Jewelry glue

Small saucer of water

tools & equipment

Pasta machine, craft oven (or a toaster oven used only for baking polymer clay), baking tile, Lisa Pavelka's UV Resin Curing Light, sharp craft scissors, craft knife, bone folder, round-nose pliers, chain-nose pliers, toothpicks

Finished length:
19" (48cm) plus 1¼" (44mm) pendant

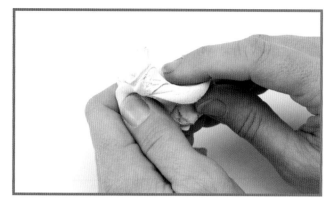

1 Condition a piece of polymer clay by rolling it between your fingers to make it more pliable.

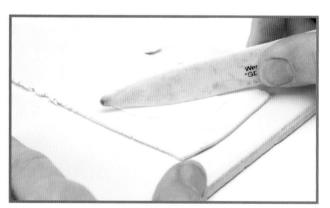

2 In the pasta machine, roll out a thin sheet a couple of millimeters thick, and place it on the baking tile.

3 Cut out a bird image from the Nunn Design collage sheet.

4 Dampen the surface of the image, press the image facedown on the pressed clay, and burnish it onto the surface using a bone folder.

5 Use your fingertip to gently rub off the paper backing immediately after burnishing. If needed, dip your fingertip in water before rubbing the paper to help loosen the fibers.

REVERSE IMAGE REVEALED
The transferred image will be the reverse of the original.

6 Press the bezel down over the transferred image to mark a cutting area.

7 Use a craft knife to cut out the impressed shape. Use an up-and-down motion while cutting; dragging the blade across the clay can tear the image.

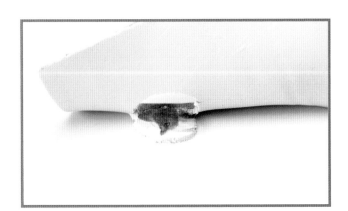

8 Carefully peel away the excess clay.

9 Test-fit the shape in the bezel and clean up the edges as needed. Then bake the clay shape in the oven for 20 minutes on the baking tile, following package instructions.

10 Squeeze UV resin onto the top of the baked clay after it has cooled. Use a toothpick to spread the resin to the outside edges.

11 Place the clay piece under the UV light for 5 minutes.

12 Glue the finished pendant into the bezel and let it dry.

13 To create the bead dangles, string each head pin with a bead, and shape the top of each wire around your round-nose pliers. Then wrap the end of each wire around the base of the loop (see *Making a wrapped loop at the end of a head pin* on page 19).

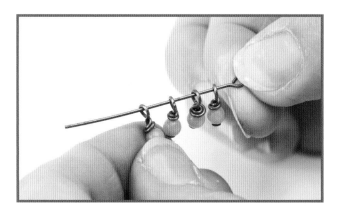

14 String all 4 dangles onto an eye pin.

15 Wrap the end of the eye pin around the round-nose pliers to shape a second eye.

16 Trim the excess wire on the eye pin.

17 Hook the eye pin onto the pendant.

18 Thread the chain through the eye pin.

19 Use jump rings to attach the clasp to the chain (see *Opening and closing a jump ring* on page 19).

CROP TO A FOCAL POINT

Compare the images on your collage sheet to your bezel selection. It's not necessary for the entire image to fit in the available bezel space; you can easily crop the background out of the image area. This project adapts well to both smaller and larger pendants.

RUN RABBIT RUN PENDANT

In the first version of this pendant, I tried to stamp the image into the uncured clay (KlayResin) and then rub alcohol inks into the impression. But the stamp got sticky in the clay, and some of the small details were lost. The inks didn't work in the impression the way I expected, but I loved the way the clay absorbed the color. So, I decided to tone the clay with ink, then stamp the beautiful natural images with permanent ink. This version is just as quick to make as the little rabbit running across the pendant.

1 Read the KlayResin package instructions, and be sure to put on your gloves (see tip sidebar). Have the bezel ready for test-fitting. Then, cut off a ¾" (19mm) section from the KlayResin roll.

2 Following package instructions, blend the clay with your fingertips. After blending, it's OK to remove your gloves.

materials

KlayResin in Porcelain White (Sherri Haab)

35mm round staple bezel (Objects and Elements)

Rabbit stamp (Pictorial Webster's Stamp Set, Flora and Fauna collection, by Chronicle Books)

Tiny leaf motif stamp (Nunn Design)

Alcohol inks: Ranger Adirondack Earthtones in Latte, Ginger and Caramel

Alcohol ink solvent (Ranger)

StazOn stamp pad: Brown

19" (48cm) velour cording

Brass fold-over crimps

Brass lobster clasp (Vintaj)

1 large (9mm) and 1 small (5mm) jump ring (Vintaj)

2 8mm unakite stone beads (Fashion Natural)

Bead cap (Vintaj)

Leaf charm (Vintaj)

Brass head pin (Vintaj)

Scrap paper

Cloth rag or old towel

basic resin supplies

Nitrile gloves, wax paper

tools

Round-nose pliers, bent-nose pliers, flush cutters, razor blade

Finished length:
19" (48cm) plus 2¾" (7cm) pendant (including dangle)

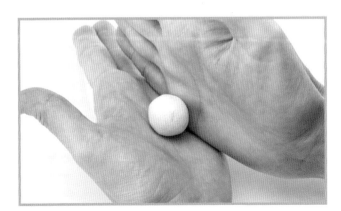

3 Once the two colors have blended into one, you need to move fast and roll the clay into a ball.

tip *It's vitally important to wear gloves while mixing the two parts of the KlayResin together. This will protect your hands while the chemical reaction is taking place. Once the material is fully mixed and stable, it's safe to remove the gloves and work with your bare hands.*

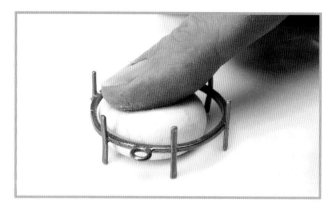

4 Center the bezel around the ball and flatten the ball so it fits comfortably inside the bezel. Remove the bezel and smooth out any rough patches. You have 3–5 minutes from the time the clay is blended to work with it before it begins drying.

5 Let the clay dry fully, which takes 12–24 hours. Then wipe the clay with a rag dipped in solvent, and apply a drop or two of pigment. The solvent helps spread the ink over the resin and dilutes its intensity.

6 With the same rag used in step 5, rub away any excess ink, so that a light base color is all that remains.

7 Ink the rabbit stamp and test-print it on scrap paper a few times to practice your technique. Be conscious of the excess color on the stamp.

8 Once you're comfortable with how to print the stamp, move to the clay piece. (If you make a mistake, use the rag dipped in alcohol ink solvent to rub off the image, then just reapply the base color and restamp.)

9 Ink the small leaf motif stamp and lightly print it in the background around the rabbit. Let the clay piece fully cure overnight.

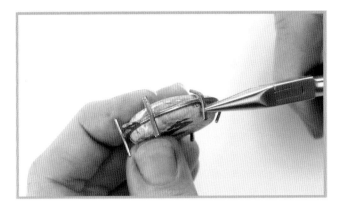

10 Reposition the cured clay piece in the bezel and use chain-nose pliers to push the staples toward the center, trapping the clay piece in place.

11 Create a bead dangle by first stringing the stone beads, followed by the bead cap, onto the head pin.

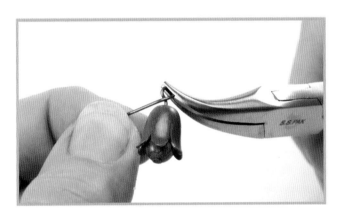

12 Form the top of the head pin into a loop around your round-nose pliers. Then wrap the wire end under the loop (see *Making a wrapped loop at the end of a head pin* on page 19).

13 Thread the dangle and the leaf charm onto a small 5mm jump ring (see *Opening and closing a jump ring* on page 19).

 tip *With this resin and bezel combination, you could easily make a double-sided design.*

14 Hook the jump ring through the base of the bezel (see *Opening and closing a jump ring* on page 19).

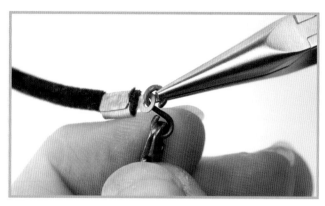

15 Hook the large 9mm jump ring through the top of the bezel (see *Opening and closing a jump ring* on page 19). Thread the velour cord through the ring.

16 Attach fold-over crimps and clasps to the cord ends (see *Folding over crimps* on page 20).

EXPERIMENT WITH SHAPES AND STAMPS

This rectangular alternative features a gorgeous owl stamp, visually balanced with added charms. Search through your stamp collection to find images for this project, and then tint the background accordingly. Vintage sailing ships stamped onto blue-gray resin could have a fabulous faux-ivory effect.

INDEX

ABOUT THE AUTHOR

This is Heidi Boyd's fourteenth title with North Light Books, and it arrives on the heels of the incredibly successful *Wired Beautiful*. Heidi creates at the dining room table where she can keep an eye on the family and dash out the door for the next carpool. Her goal is to make sophisticated design approachable and easy for all. She has a fine arts degree and got her start in professional crafting as a contributor to *Better Homes and Gardens* books and magazines. Heidi, along with her husband, Jon, their three children, and their pup, Otto, actively enjoys the natural beauty of their home in the woods of Maine.

ACKNOWLEDGMENTS

I'm a lucky gal to live with an incredibly supportive husband; without Jon's help, I wouldn't have a single book to my name. He is the love of my life, brings home the bacon, cooks up a fabulous dinner, and will drive our teenagers into the wee hours of the night. He also weighs in on my designs and helps me problem-solve mistakes.

The craft industry was completely behind this project and willingly shipped boxes of goodies to our home. I'm especially grateful for the product samples from Castin' Craft (www.eti-usa.com/category/consumer-products); ICE Resin (www.iceresin.com); Little Windows (www.little-windows.com); Sherri Haab (www.sherrihaab-shop.com); Lisa Pavelka (www.lisapavelka.com); Rings & Things (www.rings-things.com), a great online source for bezels and resin supplies; Vintaj (www.vintaj.com); and Beadalon (www.beadalon.com), who generously donated tools and stringing wires. A big shout-out to my designer friend Julie Brown-Zinchuk, who gifted me her fabulous collection of vintage jewelry and ephemera that is featured in many of the designs in this book.

I'm especially grateful for the generosity of indie crafters who answered my never-ending questions about what resin they use and why. I found inspiration in the pages of Sherri Haab's book, *The Art of Resin Jewelry*, as well as the work of Susan Lenart Kazmer, Jen Cushman, and countless other pioneers and artists in this rapidly expanding field.

DEDICATION

To my budding artist, Celia: It's my sincere wish that your creativity continues to bring you happiness and satisfaction. I also dedicate this book to crafters everywhere, who encourage me and keep me in this fabulous career. I love connecting with you on Facebook and my blog (http://heidiboyd.blogspot.com). Please continue to share your creations and questions with me.

www.fwmedia.com

16   15   14   13   12   5   4   3   2   1

DISTRIBUTED IN CANADA BY FRASER DIRECT
100 Armstrong Avenue
Georgetown, ON, Canada L7G 5S4
Tel: (905) 877-4411

DISTRIBUTED IN THE U.K. AND EUROPE BY F&W MEDIA INTERNATIONAL
Brunel House, Newton Abbot, Devon, TQ12 4PU, England
Tel: (+44) 1626 323200, Fax: (+44) 1626 323319
Email: enquiries@fwmedia.com

DISTRIBUTED IN AUSTRALIA BY CAPRICORN LINK
P.O. Box 704, S. Windsor NSW, 2756 Australia
Tel: (02) 4577-3555

SRN: W6552
ISBN-13: 978-1-4403-1872-6
ISBN-10: 1-4403-1872-7

Edited by *Stefanie Laufersweiler*
Layout design by *Emma Sandquest Design*
Cover design by *Sarah Clark*
Production by *Greg Nock*
Photography by *Marissa Bowers*, *Christine Polomsky*

metric conversion chart

To convert	to	multiply by
Inches	Centimeters	2.54
Centimeters	Inches	0.4
Feet	Centimeters	30.5
Centimeters	Feet	0.03
Yards	Meters	0.9
Meters	Yards	1.1

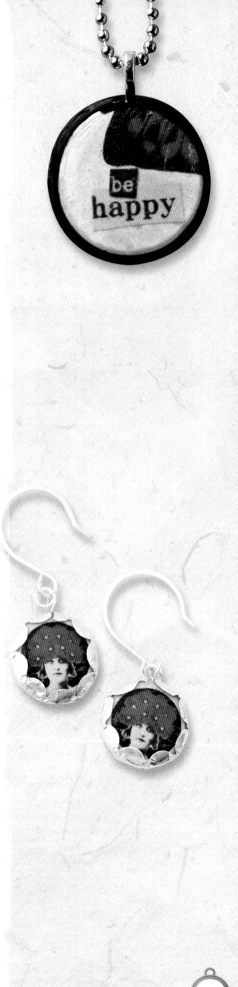

DISCOVER THE *Art* OF MAKING JEWELRY

Wired Beautiful
by Heidi Boyd
Featuring 30+ projects and a complete basic techniques section that illustrate numerous ways to use wire in your jewelry projects.

Tales of Adornment
by Kristen Robinson
Learn how to use resin to make beautifully feminine, uniquely vintage jewelry. Charming stories accompany each piece.

Semiprecious Salvage
by Stephanie Lee
Go green by incorporating found items into unique jewelry pieces such as brooches, pendants, necklaces, earrings and belts.

NORTH LIGHT BOOKS
Cincinnati, Ohio

These and other fine North Light titles are available from your local craft retailer, bookstore or online supplier, or visit our website at www.CreateMixedMedia.com.

 Follow us on Twitter at fwcraft

 Become a fan on Facebook at fwcraft